This marvelous volume is a readable, ac... of many of the questions we've always had but had not dared ask. David Robertson, with his candid, thoroughly biblical, winsome approach, reassures us that there are reasonable and convincing answers to each of them. I wish I had been given a book like this when I was a young Christian. I highly recommend it not only for teens but for all ages.

William Edgar
Professor of Apologetics,
Westminster Theological Seminary, Philadelphia

A.S.K. answers common questions asked by average teenagers from around the world. Mr Robertson candidly answers hot button questions that teens struggle with including racism, same sex marriage, and gender identity disorder. This is a helpful book that constantly points to the Bible as a lifeline on how to cope with peers, prejudice, and social media.

Esther Nixon
A high school freshmen from the United States who loves
music and playing instruments, especially piano!

I do Christian music for little kids. Kids grow up. They ask questions. Big, blunt, sharp questions that really matter. And they want straight answers they can trust. That's what this book is all about. Christian kids need God's word to shape the way they'll walk into a wide, challenging, questioning world. Time for David Robertson to lead you on, to answer your REAL WORLD questions with his brave, straight, REAL WORD answers.

Colin Buchanan
Award winning singer/songwriter

If you're a teenager trying to follow Jesus it is more than likely that you've asked most of the 52 question that David Robertson tries to answer. These are real questions and David doesn't fudge the answers. Like a friend of mine who worked with young people, he doesn't think he is the fount of all knowledge so, whatever the question, he begins by finding a Bible passage that speaks to the issue and roots his answer there. This is not just an AMA (ask me anything) session. This is; what does God's word have to say? Then when he gives his answer he asks us to pray. That's is because we're not dealing with theoretical or academic concepts. These questions are real and affect our lives. They turn us to God in worship and thanks and encourage us to bring our concerns to him.

David Robertson is real. He talks about his own experience and the struggles he has gone through. And he is never boring; always getting to the point and not confusing us with jargon. It's not going to give you easy answers but they are satisfying.

You can dip into this book or read it through. If you're serious about following Jesus it will not only strengthen your faith but it will equip you to speak confidently to others about it.

Andy Bathgate
Chief Executive, SU Scotland

The questions posed by teenagers are often more honest, practical and down-to-earth than the average adult. David Robertson takes them seriously by being just as straight-talking and practical in response. Young people, youth leaders and parents will all be helped by the wide range of issues tackled in this timely book.

Justin Brierley
Premier Christian Radio Presenter

A.S.K.

REAL WORLD QUESTIONS / REAL WORD ANSWERS

DAVID ROBERTSON

TRUTHFORLIFE®

CF4·K

10 9 8 7 6 5 4 3

Copyright © David Robertson 2019

Paperback ISBN 978-1-5271-0585-0
epub ISBN 978-1-5271-0394-8
mobi ISBN 978-1-5271-0395-5

Published in 2019
Reprinted 2019
This edition published in 2020
by Christian Focus Publications, Ltd.
Geanies House, Fearn,
Ross-shire, IV20 1TW, Scotland.
www.christianfocus.com

with

Truth for Life
P.O. Box 398000
Cleveland, Ohio 44139
truthforlife.org

Cover and page design by Moose77.com

Printed in the U.S.A.

This book is dedicated to the young people of St Peter's Free Church, Dundee, the Youth group of St Thomas' Anglican Church in Sydney and the young people from all over the world who helped me with this book. It is for you ... and for my grandchildren – Isla, Finlay and Evie – who I hope will one day be able to read it!

INTRODUCTION

Welcome to A.S.K – Ask. Seek. Knock. These words are from Jesus:

'Ask and it will be given to you; seek and you will find; knock and the door will be opened to you. For everyone who asks receives; the one who seeks finds; and to the one who knocks, the door will be opened' (Matthew 7:7-8).

This book deals with the first part of that promise from Jesus – Ask. We all have questions about Jesus, the Bible, the Christian faith and our culture today. The great news is that Jesus gives answers. The questions in this book were gathered from teenagers in fifteen countries in five different continents. All of them are real questions from real teenagers – with the exception of a couple of grammatical and spelling corrections they are as I was sent them. I received hundreds so I have tried to take a representative sample covering most of the main issues.

The format is very simple. There are fifty-two short chapters. Each contains a question, a Bible passage, a Bible verse, a discussion, something to consider, recommended further reading and a prayer.

This book is written for 15-17 year olds who are already Christians or who have grown up in a Christian home or go to church, who have questions. But I also hope it will prove helpful to those who are not yet Christians and those who are older and younger. It is designed to be used either individually or as part of a youth group, school or church. The further recommended reading is not a requirement! It's just a suggestion for follow up on any particular question that you are especially interested in. Some of the books are quite hard-going, others are much easier ... but my view is that every teenager has a brain ... they just need to use them! If you are the kind of person who doesn't like reading, or struggles with it, I hope that you will manage this book! The chapters are short, but there is a lot packed in them. If you want more – excellent – this book is not intended to be the definitive answer on any of the questions here. Think of them as discussion starters.

My aim is to try to get us all to think biblically about these issues, to pray and to worship. My 'answers' may result in further questions – I hope they will. But I hope even more that you will come to see and know better the one who is the answer. Jesus Christ. May we all be his disciples!

David Robertson

CONTENTS

Introduction / **7**

1. God Speaks *(1 Samuel 3)* / **11**
2. Trusting the Bible *(2 Timothy 3:10-17)* / **15**
3. God's Unchanging Word *(1 Timothy 1:1-11)* / **19**
4. Helping God *(Psalm 116)* / **23**
5. Harry Potter *(Luke 1:1-25)* / **27**
6. Blasphemy Against the Holy Spirit *(Mark 3:20-35)* / **31**
7. The Big Bang *(Genesis 1:1-23)* / **35**
8. Science, Knowledge and God *(Romans 1:18-23)* / **39**
9. Finding God *(Job 11)* / **43**
10. The Uncreated God *(Isaiah 40:21-31)* / **47**
11. The Gender of God *(Numbers 23:1-26)* / **51**
12. The Trinity *(Matthew 28)* / **55**
13. The Mind of God *(1 Corinthians 2:6-16)* / **59**
14. God and Suffering *(Psalm 119:65-72)* / **63**
15. The Death of Jesus *(John 3:14-21)* / **67**
16. Jesus – the Only Saviour *(Acts 4:1-12)* / **71**
17. Forgiveness *(Hebrews 9:11-28)* / **75**
18. Hell *(Isaiah 30:8-18)* / **79**
19. The Certainty of Heaven *(1 John 5:11-21)* / **83**
20. Animals in Heaven *(Psalm 104:24-35)* / **87**
21. Suicide *(Judges 16:23-31)* / **91**
22. Those who have not heard *(Genesis 18:16-33)* / **95**
23. The End of the World *(2 Peter 3:1-18)* / **99**
24. Reincarnation *(John 5:16-30)* / **103**
25. The Purpose of Life *(Ephesians 2:1-10)* / **107**
26. Rich and Famous *(1 Timothy 6:3-21)* / **111**
27. Being a Christian *(Acts 11:19-30)* / **115**

28.   Religion and Birth *(John 1:1-18)* / **119**

29.   Hitler *(Ezekiel 18)* / **123**

30.   Racism *(Acts 17:16-34)* / **127**

31.   North Korea *(Isaiah 40:1-20)* / **131**

32.   Division and Peace *(Ephesians 2:11-22)* / **135**

33.   Sex and Same Sex Marriage *(1 Thessalonians 4:1-8)* / **139**

34.   Pornography *(Matthew 5:27-30)* / **143**

35.   Islam and Love *(Matthew 5:38-48)* / **147**

36.   Transgender *(Genesis 1:24-31)* / **151**

37.   Loving Yourself *(Leviticus 19:1-18)* / **155**

38.   Feeling God is Far Away *(Psalm 13)* / **159**

39.   The Trinity, Prayer and Exams *(1 Peter 5:8-11)* / **163**

40.   Why Pray? *(James 5:13-20)* / **167**

41.   Worry *(Matthew 6:24-34)* / **171**

42.   Christian Community and the Internet *(Hebrews 10:19-25)* / **175**

43.   Cool Christianity *(1 Corinthians 1:18-31)* / **179**

44.   Backsliding *(1 John 1)* / **183**

45.   Help – My Girlfriend's Pregnant! *(John 8:1-15)* / **187**

46.   Tattoos and Alcohol *(1 Corinthians 6:12-20)* / **191**

47.   Buddhist Parents *(Mark 7:1-13)* / **195**

48.   Mental Illness *(Isaiah 42:1-17)* / **199**

49.   The Role of the Law *(Galatians 3:1-14)* / **203**

50.   Church, Salvation and Hypocrisy *(Acts 2:42-47)* / **207**

51.   The Best Church *(Ephesians 4:1-16)* / **211**

52.   Knowing God's Will and Love *(Romans 12:1-21)* / **215**

And Finally / **219**

Appendix - Recommended Books / **221**

1. GOD SPEAKS

QUESTION: If God talked to Samuel, when he was a boy, why can't he talk to me? How should you go about reading the Bible? At what age am I ready to be called by God as a youth?

BIBLE READING: 1 Samuel 3

TEXT: The LORD came and stood there, calling as at the other times, 'Samuel! Samuel!' Then Samuel said, 'Speak, for your servant is listening' (1 Samuel 3:10).

Wouldn't things be so much easier if God just spoke directly to us? Some people say that he does. They hear his voice all the time. You hear them say things like 'God told me to do this', or 'God told me to marry that person'. Wouldn't life be so much better if we could have God like some kind of spiritual Google – answering our questions whenever we asked? A sort of spiritual slot machine where you put in the prayer and out comes the answer. Instead of asking 'Siri', 'Echo' or 'Google', we could just ask God.

But that's not how it works. Often when people say 'God told me', what they really mean is; 'this is what I felt or thought'. But our feelings and thoughts are not really the best guideline for knowing the will of God are they?

Imagine you were Samuel. A teenage boy living in Israel, taken away from your mother and father, to live in the temple and serve with the old priest Eli. Life would be quite confusing. You see things done in the temple by Eli's sons, Hophni and Phineas, which you know are wrong. Things are not good. Wouldn't it be great if God could speak to you? And then one night you are lying down in the house of the LORD and you hear a voice calling you by name. You think it is Eli and so you run to him. But it isn't him and so you go back to bed. Three times this happens – and then Eli understands what is going on and he tells you that the next time you hear the voice you should reply, 'Speak LORD, for your servant is listening.' How would you feel lying there? I think I would be pretty scared.

When God called Samuel again, he said the words he had been told, and God then revealed what was going to happen to Eli. This was not the normal way for God to speak to his people then (look at verse 1: 'In those days the word of the LORD was rare; there were not many visions'); and it is not the normal way today. Hebrews 1:1-2 says:

'In the past God spoke to our ancestors through the prophets at many times and in various ways, but in these last days he has spoken to us by his Son, whom he appointed heir of all things, and through whom also he made the universe.'

Verse 7 tells us that Samuel did not yet know the LORD because the Word of the LORD had not yet been revealed to him. Just like Samuel we need God's Word to be revealed to us

– because that is how we know the Word, Jesus Christ. We are told that the LORD was with Samuel as he grew up and he will be with you as you commit yourself to him and follow Jesus as he is revealed in his Word.

HOW SHOULD WE READ THE BIBLE? As the Word of God. Precious. Valuable. The greatest treasure you will ever find. We should study and pray as we realise that it is a real and living Word. Even more certain than if God spoke to us with a visible voice or in a dream. The Bible brings us Jesus. This is the great thing about the Bible. Peter tells us that we have the 'word of the prophets made more certain' or completely reliable, and that we would do well to pay attention to it, as a light shining in a dark place (1 Peter 2:19). You don't have to rely on your feelings, or have a vision. Nor is the Word of the LORD 'rare' in our day. We have it given to us in the Bible. What a wonderful gift.

WHEN ARE WE READY TO BE CALLED BY GOD AS A YOUTH? Now. When you hear and understand the Word of God. When you know who Jesus is and hear him calling you to believe and trust in him, then you are being called to repent, confess your sins and turn to him. You are never too young! We are told that Samuel as a young person 'ministered' before the Lord. You are called to belong to him and to serve (minister before) him. Beginning now!

CONSIDER: When do you read the Bible? By yourself and with others. How much do you value God's great gift to us?

RECOMMENDED FURTHER READING:

From the Mouth of God – Sinclair B. Ferguson

PRAYER: Lord Jesus, I thank you that you spoke to Samuel when he was so young and I thank you that you still speak to young people today through your living and enduring Word. I thank you that the Bible is certain and I pray that you would reveal yourself and your will to me through your Word. Amen.

2. TRUSTING THE BIBLE

QUESTION: How do you know you can trust the Bible? Why should I care about a really, really, really old book? It can't be relevant today, can it?

BIBLE READING: 2 Timothy 3:10-17

TEXT: But as for you, continue in what you have learned and have become convinced of, because you know those from whom you learned it, and how from infancy you have known the Holy Scriptures, which are able to make you wise for salvation through faith in Christ Jesus. All Scripture is God-breathed and is useful for teaching, rebuking, correcting and training in righteousness, so that the servant of God may be thoroughly equipped for every good work (2 Timothy 3:14-17).

Trust is really important. If we don't trust someone then we won't believe what they say. This is even more important when it comes to things that are really vital to our lives. If you

15

are a delivery driver and you have to travel to an area you do not know, you need a reliable map or Sat Nav. If you are a doctor you need to have a good and trustworthy list of the appropriate drugs to use. The Bible is even more important than that. If it is to reveal Jesus to us, show us the way to heaven, tell us about ourselves and give us guidelines for our lives, then it had better be accurate!

Some people who are not Christians will argue that the Bible cannot be the Word of God. That's because they don't believe in God, and therefore he cannot have a word. To them a non-existent being clearly does not speak. The trouble is that they have usually made their minds up without any evidence.

Some people are what we call 'chronological snobs'. A 'place snob' is someone who thinks that just because of the place they live in, they are a better person. A chronological snob is a time snob. They think that just because they live in the twenty-first century they are better than every one who has gone before. But think about that! Just as living in the U.S.A. or the U.K. does not make you a better person than someone who lives in Africa or China; so living in the twenty-first century does not make you a better person than someone who lived in the first century.

Being really old might actually be much better. Imagine if you as a young person said: 'I'm not going to listen to older people, because they are older'. Would that not be a pretty arrogant and stupid thing to do? Older people generally will have more experience and you could have a lot to learn from them. Similarly, to dismiss the Bible because it is old would be both arrogant and stupid.

However, just because something is old, does not mean it is right. So how do we know we can trust the Bible? There are lots of different reasons ... the evidence of those who have been helped by the Bible, the witness of those who have taught it to us, the fact that it has stood the test of time, the beauty and truth within it, the way that we experience it today. But the only way we really know is when the author, the Holy Spirit, bears witness in our heart's using his Word, to show us that it really is the Word of God.

I became a Christian when I was about sixteen years old. I have been studying and reading and teaching the Bible for forty years since then. And I can honestly tell you that I have found it to be 100 per cent reliable (although not always easy!) and always 100 per cent relevant to wherever I have been. The Bible is relevant. We don't need to make it relevant. Indeed, when we try to do so by changing it, we always end up making it irrelevant.

We can trust the Word of God, because it is the Word of God. It is 'God-breathed'. Inspired by the Holy Spirit as Peter tells us:

'For prophecy never had its origin in the human will, but prophets, though human, spoke from God as they were carried along by the Holy Spirit' (2 Peter 1:21).

God does not lie. Jesus does not lie. The Holy Spirit does not lie. It is the devil who is the father of lies. He is the one who always seeks to undermine the Bible so that we will not trust our God.

CONSIDER: Do you trust the Bible? Who do you ask if you have any questions? How do you think the devil tries to stop us listening to God speaking to us through his Word?

RECOMMENDED FURTHER READING:
Why Trust the Bible – Amy Orr-Ewing

PRAYER: Our Father in heaven, we bless you that you have given us your Word; that you have breathed it out; that you inspired the prophets and apostles to record and bring it to us. And we thank you that your Word is as sure today as it ever was. Heaven and earth will pass away, but your Word is eternal. Thank you for the certainty it brings to us. Enable us to understand and apply it. In Jesus' name. Amen.

3. GOD'S UNCHANGING WORD

QUESTION: Nowadays Christians think that things like adultery and slavery are sins, but in Abraham's time it was socially acceptable to have two wives as well as slaves and God doesn't correct this? So does God adapt to social norms? Do sins evolve with culture? Or does God simply not count?

BIBLE READING: 1 Timothy 1:1-11

TEXT: We know that the law is good if one uses it properly. We also know that the law is made not for the righteous but for lawbreakers and rebels, the ungodly and sinful, the unholy and irreligious, for those who kill their fathers or mothers, for murderers, for the sexually immoral, for those practicing homosexuality, for slave traders and liars and perjurers—and for whatever else is contrary to the sound doctrine that conforms to the gospel concerning the glory of the blessed God, which he entrusted to me (1 Timothy 1:8-11).

This is a great and important question. It is also one that is asked a lot – not least because there are parts of the Bible that seem, in the light of our culture, to be horrific.

Do you know what the word 'zeitgeist' means? It refers to the mood, spirit or understanding of a particular time or culture. Can we judge people from another culture and another era by the values of ours? The answer really has to be no. We can't. But the Christian has a different perspective because we believe that every era and every culture can and should be judged by God. This is where the problem behind the question lies. It's not that God does not count – it's more that there seems to be a change in standards. But is this really the case? God's character does not change. He is always holy, glorious, good, loving and just. His law, based upon his character, does not change – murder is always wrong. Rape is always wrong. Stealing is always wrong. Racism is always wrong. False worship is always wrong. Sin is sin.

I don't think that there is a change in standards. It's just that God reveals himself and his will gradually. It's a bit like a curtain being pulled back slowly and the light being gradually let in. It's what we call 'progressive revelation'. God's law reveals more and more of his standards and as it does so, it shows up our sin and the sins of our culture. Paul gives an example of us when he speaks to the philosophers in Athens:

'In the past God overlooked such ignorance, but now he commands all people everywhere to repent. For he has set a day when he will judge the world with justice by the man he has appointed. He has given proof of this to everyone by raising him from the dead' (Acts 17:30-31).

You see that everything leads up to Jesus.

As Paul tells the young man, Timothy, in today's passage 'the law is good if one uses it properly'.

There is also another principle called 'accommodation'. When God communicates with us he needs to accommodate himself to us, so that we can understand and apply what is being said. Accommodation also means that God reveals himself in the context of our culture and seeks to change it through his Word. It is evolution not revolution.

It is also an important principle to remember when we are reading the Bible that much of what we read is descriptive (describing what happened) and not prescriptive (telling us what should happen). For example, when we read about Jephthah sacrificing his daughter, that is not a command for fathers to do likewise today!

Let's see how this works out in terms of slavery. Some people think that the Bible condones slavery. I don't. I think it regulates it in cultures where it was practiced, (Abraham's and the Greco/Roman culture in which the New Testament was written) but the teaching of the Bible as a whole is against the idea and practice of slavery. So in the passage we read we find that slave traders are guilty of breaking God's law ... if there are no slave traders, there will soon be no slaves!

You also need to remember that the Bible is not primarily a law book, or a 'how to' book. It is a revelation both of God and a description of the sinfulness of humanity and the remedy that God has provided to deal with that sin. The fact that God accommodates himself to us in order to reveal his glory and lead us to repent of our sin, does not mean that God approves of our sin.

At the end of the day, Paul gives us a great standard here. Everything must conform to the sound doctrine that conforms to the gospel concerning the glory of the blessed God. Once you get that as the big picture, the smaller details will fall into place.

CONSIDER: What do you think would have happened if we had been given all God's law at once and told to obey it immediately or be destroyed? Why do you think God gradually revealed the gospel?

RECOMMENDED FURTHER READING:
God's Big Picture – Vaughan Roberts

PRAYER: Lord God, we thank you for the wisdom in your Word. We thank you that over hundreds of years, you gradually revealed your will and Word, until the final Word, Jesus Christ came. We bless you that he is the bigger picture and once we read your Word in his light – it becomes so much clearer. Help us to understand and apply it today in our culture, in the name of Jesus. Amen.

4. HELPING GOD

QUESTION: The Bible says, 'God helps those who help themselves'. What are the good and bad ways of helping God?

BIBLE READING: Psalm 116

TEXT: What shall I return to the LORD for all his goodness to me? (Psalm 116:12)

People will often cite the Bible as their authority for a saying ... when the Bible says nothing of the sort. For example if your mother ever says to you; 'the Bible says, cleanliness is next to godliness' as she urges you to make your bed, then you can politely and graciously tell her that whilst you agree making your bed is important and you will do it, the Bible doesn't actually say that! Likewise with the saying, 'God helps those who help themselves'. That is not in the Bible – nor indeed anything like it – because in fact it goes against the teaching of the Bible.

I find it quite interesting where this phrase comes from. It is found in two of Aesop's fables and a variation of it is also in the Quran.

'Indeed God will not change the conditions of a population until they change what is in themselves' (Quran 13:11).

What's wrong with this way of thinking? And why are we glad it's not in the Bible? Because it would leave God as weak and pathetic – not an Almighty God, but someone who needed our help. This might feel good to start with – after all isn't it nice when someone asks for and needs our help? Except when we are unable to help! The God of the Bible is all-powerful and sovereign. Paul told the philosophers in Athens:

'*The God who made the world and everything in it is the Lord of heaven and earth and does not live in temples built by human hands. And he is not served by human hands, as if he needed anything. Rather, he himself gives everyone life and breath and everything else*' (Acts 17:24-25).

God does not *need* our help. On the other hand we desperately need him. It is in him that we live and move and have our being. Without God we cannot live, learn or love. God is good and the giver of all things good. We cannot add to him – or make up what he lacks. Psalm 116 tells of a man in a desperate situation. He is on the edge of death, entangled by its cords. He is terrified and overcome with distress and sorrow. He calls out to the Lord: 'Lord, save me!' He doesn't say, 'Look, Lord, I'll do you a deal. You help me and I'll help you a bit ... we need each other'.

Then he finds that the Lord is gracious, righteous and full of compassion. God saves him. God rescues the weary. He helps the helpless.

Then and only then does the psalmist say what he will do for God.

'*What shall I return to the LORD for all his goodness to me? I will lift up the cup of salvation and call on the name of the LORD. I will fulfil my vows to the LORD in the presence of all his people*' (Psalm 116:12-14).

What does that mean for you and me? It means that when we have become aware of our helplessness and called on the name of the Lord, we are saved. When we are saved, we are thankful. When we are thankful we serve. We move from sin to salvation to serving. To reverse that and try to serve so that we can earn salvation will only lead to more sin.

This is the great news of the Good News of Jesus. He has paid it all. Now we have been set free. Some people think that this means we are free to sin, or that we can do whatever we want and don't need to actually do anything for God because he will just give us anything we want. But that is not what Christian freedom is. We are set free to serve the living God.

There is, however, a sense in which this saying *is* true. The English general, Oliver Cromwell, is supposed to have said before the battle of Edgehill in 1642, 'Trust in God and keep your powder dry.' What he meant was that just because we trust in God, it doesn't mean that we are not to act, work or take precautions ourselves. Rather it is *because* we trust in God that we can work.

CONSIDER: Do you know your own helplessness? Do you know God's salvation? If so, what are you doing in grateful response for that? How are you serving the Living God?

RECOMMENDED FURTHER READING:
Serving without Sinking – John Hindley

PRAYER: O Lord, we thank you that you hear the cries of the helpless. We are helpless and we need to find our rest in you. O Lord, grant us your salvation, give us life and make us your willing, serving children from now on. Amen.

5. HARRY POTTER

BIBLE READING: Luke 1:1-25

TEXT: Many have undertaken to draw up an account of the things that have been fulfilled among us, just as they were handed down to us by those who from the first were eyewitnesses and servants of the word. With this in mind, since I myself have carefully investigated everything from the beginning, I too decided to write an orderly account for you, most excellent Theophilus, so that you may know the certainty of the things you have been taught (Luke 1:1-4).

The Harry Potter series of books are incredibly popular all over the world. They have been translated into eighty languages and have sold over 500 million copies! They are well-written and tell some great stories ... children and young people (and a lot of adults) love them.

Some Christians think that they are of the devil, because they speak of magic and spells. I edit a magazine and

I remember when one of the books came out I asked my teenage daughter, Becky, if she would write a review. She queued up at the local bookshop for the midnight opening (she was, and is, a big fan!), read the book within twenty-four hours and had the review for me the next day. I think we were the first Christian magazine to have a review of Harry Potter! And some people complained. Was this not promoting witchcraft? Not at all! Not unless you are prepared to condemn the fairy tales of the Brothers Grimm, the Narnia tales and *The Lord of the Rings*!

At the opposite extreme are those who regard the Harry Potter books as some kind of Christian analogy. They are not that either. Although J.K. Rowling is a member of the Church of Scotland and claims 'Christianity inspired Harry Potter'.[1] Spoiler alert! In the last book the hero is resurrected from the dead after dying in sacrifice for everyone else. And there are other Christian parallels. So the answer to your question is yes and no. It's a great story, inspired by Christianity in some ways, but it is not based on the Bible.

But what about this idea? What if all great stories throughout the world are reflections of the greatest story of all – the story of the Bible and above all the story of Jesus? I think that is true – but the other thing that you need to remember and always keep in mind is that the Bible is not a made up story. It is not a myth. It is the real story of Jesus.

In this week's passage Dr Luke tells us how he came to write his Gospel (and the book of Acts). He doesn't begin with 'once upon a time', or 'there was a hobbit who lived in a hole'. He begins like a historian – telling us where he got his sources, (the eyewitnesses of Jesus) and what he did, and how he 'carefully

---

1. From an article by Jonathan Petre, Religion Correspondent 20 Oct, 2007.

investigated everything from the beginning'. He then decides to write down everything for a person called Theophilus (the name means 'loved of God' and since Luke calls him 'most excellent' – he was probably a Roman official or high up Roman citizen), so that he would be certain of things about Jesus he had been taught.

That's the difference between Harry Potter and the Bible. Harry Potter is a made-up story that was at least partly inspired by the Bible. However, the Bible is the inspired Word of God, which tells us the *real* story about Jesus. You can enjoy reading Harry Potter, but you cannot base your life on it. You can enjoy reading the Bible – and it is essential that you base your life upon what you learn in it.

CONSIDER: Do you think it is good to read stories, other than those in the Bible? Why? What are the good things we can get from such stories? What are the possible dangers?

RECOMMENDED FURTHER READING:
http://www.beliefnet.com/entertainment/books/galleries/5-ways-harry-potter-mirrors-the-christian-story.aspx?p=2

Looking for God in Harry Potter – John Granger

PRAYER: Lord Jesus, thank you for the gift of storytelling, and the gift of great writers. Thank you, most of all, for those your Holy Spirit inspired to write your story. We pray that we would never be distracted from the greatest story of all and that we would not live our lives in a fantasy world, but rather in your reality. Amen.

6. BLASPHEMY AGAINST THE HOLY SPIRIT

QUESTION: I think I've blasphemed the Holy Spirit. What hope is there for me?

BIBLE READING: Mark 3:20-35

TEXT: Truly I tell you, people can be forgiven all their sins and every slander they utter, but whoever blasphemes against the Holy Spirit will never be forgiven; they are guilty of an eternal sin (Mark 3:28-29).

This is a really tough and scary question. I know how you feel. Many years ago I was hitchhiking through Europe as a sixteen-year-old, with one of my friends. We managed to survive and get back to London, where a friend invited us to a church meeting in a YMCA. At first it seemed fine – if a bit lively! But then it got really weird. People all around seemed to be babbling (I understood later that it was called 'speaking in tongues'). I was a bit freaked out about it – and I was especially concerned for my friend, who was not a Christian. I was worried that he would think we were all mad! So, because it was an open meeting where anyone could speak, I stood up and read from my Bible.

'When you pray, do not keep babbling like pagans, for they think they will be heard because of their many words' (Matthew 6:7).

There was a stunned silence and then it got even weirder. People gathered round me, 'laid hands' on me, someone 'prophesied' and thanked God that 'this thorn was being turned into a rose'! We got out of there as quickly as possible! I didn't feel very rosy!

The next day the leader of the group asked to see me. He then told me one of the cruellest things you could ever say to a young Christian – 'You have blasphemed against the Holy Spirit.' For two years I was really concerned that I had committed the unforgivable sin – until a wise, older Christian met with me, and told me that if I had committed the unforgivable sin, I wouldn't be bothered about it, because my heart would be so hard.

I don't know what sin it is you think you have committed when you are concerned about having 'blasphemed against the Holy Spirit'. But let me assure you that every sin is forgivable – even the most horrendous ones.

'If we claim to be without sin, we deceive ourselves and the truth is not in us. If we confess our sins, he is faithful and just and will forgive us our sins and purify us from all unrighteousness' (1 John 1:8-9).

So what is the blasphemy against the Holy Spirit?

It is the deliberate shutting of our hearts and minds to the witness of the Spirit about Jesus. That is what the Pharisees were doing. It is when we know that the gospel is true, when we experience its power and yet still refuse to come to Christ – and so remain as a non-Christian for the rest of our days.

Before I became a Christian I was conscious of God working in my life and speaking through his Word to me. But I didn't want to become a Christian. I thought it would be too hard – or that I could do it later. But there came a time when I knew both that it was true and that this time could be the last time. I knew that God had said, 'my Spirit will not always strive with man' and I knew that it would be wrong of me to turn away from Jesus. I guess if I had continued to do that throughout my life, I would have committed the one unforgivable sin – the blasphemy against the Holy Spirit.

Maybe you are bothered and worried that that is what you have done. But the reason you can be certain you haven't, is the very fact that you *are* bothered. If you were hardened against God, you couldn't care less. But you do care.

Whatever it is that is bothering you, whatever it is that you feel God cannot forgive you for, don't hold back. Take it to him. Just look back at what we read from John and believe God's Word – not your own fears. He is faithful and just and will forgive us for ALL unrighteousness. What a wonderful and marvellous freedom that is!

CONSIDER: It is good to confess our sins, specifically as well as generally. If you are worried about this particular sin, ask God to show you his mercy. Think about what other sins you might want to confess. Pray that God would show you your sin, and lead you in the way everlasting.

RECOMMENDED FURTHER READING:

Psalms – The Prayer Book of the Bible – Dietrich Bonhoeffer

PRAYER: Search me, God, and know my heart;
test me and know my anxious thoughts.
See if there is any offensive way in me,
and lead me in the way everlasting (Psalm 139:23-24).

7. THE BIG BANG

QUESTION: Why doesn't Christianity accept the Big Bang theory?

BIBLE READING: Genesis 1:1-23

TEXT: In the beginning God created the heavens and the earth. Now the earth was formless and empty, darkness was over the surface of the deep, and the Spirit of God was hovering over the waters (Genesis 1:1-2).

One of the big problems that many young people face is when they are told something is what 'Christianity' teaches – when it is nothing of the sort. Just as we must not take away from the Bible – so we must not add to it. Some Christians express far more certainty based upon their interpretations than they do upon the Bible itself.

This question reflects that. Because it is based upon the wrong premise – that Christianity does not accept the Big Bang theory. Of course it all depends on what we mean by 'Big Bang theory'. If you mean that the Universe started all by itself with a Big Bang then of course that idea is not only unbiblical but it is foolish. But if you mean that when God created the universe he did so with a Big Bang – there is no problem!

Some Christians don't like it because it suggests a universe billions of years old. And they believe that the Bible teaches that the universe is only a few thousand years old. This is an area where Bible-believing Christians disagree.

So let's ask first of all what the Big Bang theory is. It states that the universe had a beginning and that that beginning was, a Big Bang! This is a big improvement on the general scientific consensus in the first half of the twentieth century which stated that the universe was eternal and had no beginning. But then the scientists caught up with the Bible and because of the discovery of the Big Bang, they came to realise that Genesis 1:1 was after all correct. There was a beginning.

Then let's think about it from a Christian perspective. God spoke and the universe came into being. Do you think he did it with a whimper, or with awesome power?! So there is really no contradiction between the Bible and the idea that the Universe began with a bang. I don't see why you can't believe both.

But what about the age of the universe? Again the Bible doesn't really have anything to say on this. Look at our verses again. God created the heavens and the earth out of nothing. The universe was formless and void before he then went on to the sequence of creation described in Genesis 1.

I am not a scientist but I have read a lot about what scientists have said about this. For example, Arno Penzias, the Nobel Prize winning scientist who discovered the background radiation that proved the Big Bang stated:

---

2. *New York Times*, March 12, 1978.

'The best data we have are exactly what I would have predicted, had I nothing to go on but the five books of Moses, the Psalms, the Bible as a whole.'[2]

Then Robert Jastrow, an Astrophysicist, writes,

'Now we see how the astronomical evidence leads to a biblical view of the origin of the world. The details differ, but the essential elements and the astronomical and biblical accounts of Genesis are the same; the chain of events leading to man commenced suddenly and sharply at a definite moment in time, in a flash of light and energy.'[3]

Another top scientist confesses,

'I am personally persuaded that a super-intelligent Creator exists beyond and within the cosmos, and that the rich context of congeniality shown by our universe, permitting and encouraging the existence of self-conscious life, is part of the Creator's design and purpose'[4] (Owen Gingerich, God's Universe).

Even the atheist scientist, Stephen Hawking, wrote in his most famous book, A Brief History of Time:

'It would be very difficult to explain why the universe should have begun in just this way, except as the act of a God who intended to create beings like us.'[5]

It is very difficult. Which is why his book is so hard to read – because he tries to explain away the obvious. It's amazing that the heavens declare the glory of God, that the creation testifies to the Creator, and yet such is the blindness of human beings, that even the cleverest shut their eyes and refuse to see.

---

3. *God and the Astronomers*, Robert Jastrow, Norton, 1978.

4. *God's Universe*, Owen Gingerich, Harvard University Press, 2006.

5. *A Brief History of Time*, Stephen Hawking, Bantam Dell Publishing Group, 1988.

It's not Christians who deny the Big Bang. We affirm the one who created through the Big Bang. It's non-Christians who have the enormous difficulties of trying to explain what banged and who did the banging!

CONSIDER: Stephen Hawking points out that if the rate of expansion, one second after the Big Bang, had been smaller by even one part in ten thousand million million, the universe would have re-collapsed before it ever reached its present state. If it had been greater by one part in a million then the stars and planets would not have been able to form. Constants like the speed of light, the force of gravity and electromagnetism all need to work precisely together for there to be life. There are fifteen such constants. Do you really think that this all just happened by chance? Is it not more likely that such an intricate and complex creation had a Creator?

RECOMMENDED FURTHER READING:
Seven Days that Shook the Earth – John Lennox

PRAYER: The heavens declare the glory of God;
    the skies proclaim the work of his hands.
    Day after day they pour forth speech;
    night after night they reveal knowledge
    They have no speech, they use no words;
    no sound is heard from them.
    Yet their voice goes out into all the earth,
    their words to the ends of the world (Psalm 19:1-4).

O Lord, help us to listen and to see your glory revealed in your creation. Amen.

8. SCIENCE, KNOWLEDGE AND GOD

QUESTION: Why do you believe in miracles and supernatural things when science can give us certain knowledge of the world? Can it be proved scientifically God exists?

BIBLE READING: Romans 1:18-23

TEXT: For since the creation of the world God's invisible qualities—his eternal power and divine nature—have been clearly seen, being understood from what has been made, so that people are without excuse (Romans 1:20).

The devil is the father of lies. Lying is the way he operates. He tries to separate us from the Father of truth by causing us to doubt God's Word. In this regard one of his greatest and most successful lies is that science and Christianity are opposed.

It is really important that when we use words we know what they mean – and what others mean when they use them.

Science is the study of what God has created. Christianity is the faith based upon what God has revealed in his Word – especially about Jesus, his Son. God has given us two books – the book of nature and the book of Scripture. They don't contradict each other.

The question also implies that, whereas science gives us certain knowledge of the world, the Bible doesn't. But that is to misunderstand both science and the Bible. Science works on a principle of falsifiability – if there is no possibility of testing it for falseness then it can't be called science. It's a great method of working and finding out knowledge. But it isn't always 'certain' and even more importantly there are lots of things that science does not tell us – and will never be able to tell us. For example, if you are boiling a kettle, science can tell you how the electricity works, and what temperature causes the water to boil, but it cannot tell you why the kettle was being boiled in the first place (you want to make a cup of tea for your granny). In other words science is great at answering the 'what' questions, but not so good at answering the 'why' questions.

The Bible is not a science textbook – but it is a revelation of the God of science. All wisdom is found in Jesus Christ. Our verse tells us that whilst science might tell us about nature, nature tells us about God – and the Bible tells us what God says. There is no contradiction. Science and the Bible are not two opposed ways of knowing – they are complementary ways of knowing.

So can it be proved scientifically that God exists? The answer is both yes and no. Everything about the creation, points us to the Creator. In that sense the answer is yes. But if you are asking it in the way that so many atheists do – 'Can you put God in a test tube and conduct an experiment to prove he exists?' – the answer is no.

I once heard Professor David Wilkinson of the University of Durham speaking at the University of St Andrews on the subject of God and the universe. He was asked, 'Are you saying that science *proves* God?' He answered, 'No ... I am saying that science *points* to God'. Just as nature points to God so does science.

Let me give you one example that comes from Professor John Lennox. The human genome, the genetic code in each human cell, contains 23 DNA molecules each containing from 500 thousand to 2.5 million-nucleotide pairs. DNA molecules of this size are about 5 cm on average.

You have about 10 trillion cells in your body, so if you stretched the DNA in all the cells out, end to end, they'd go for around 750 million miles. The sun is 93,000,000 miles away, so your DNA would reach there and back about four times! What's equally amazing is that all this DNA consists of four building blocks, A, T, C and G. And every human genome is unique. In other words we are all made of this information.

It's such an amazing code. Lennox asks:

'If you went down to the beach and saw the words 'I love you' written in sea shells on the shore – would you just assume that they had been washed up by the waves, or would you think that someone had done the arranging? The answer is obvious. Given that the human DNA code is a million times more complex than that, why should there not be an equally obvious answer as to why we have such a code? The glories of God are seen as much in the human genome as they are in the billions of stars!'

CONSIDER: Given the overwhelming evidence for a Creator, why do you think some people refuse to believe in him? What does Romans 1 give as the reason why people ignore the evidence? Why is knowing that there is a Creator, not enough to save us?

RECOMMENDED FURTHER READING:
God's Undertaker – John Lennox

PRAYER: Lord God, you are the Creator of heaven and earth. You are the one who made the billions of stars beyond me, and the billions of cells within. I am fearfully and wonderfully made. Help me to marvel at your works and to worship you the Creator, rather than the creation. For your glory. Amen.

9. FINDING GOD

QUESTION: If God really wants a relationship with me, why doesn't he show himself clearer?

BIBLE READING: Job 11

TEXT: Can you fathom the mysteries of God?
   Can you probe the limits of the Almighty? (Job 11:7)

It's so simple isn't it? If only God made himself clear then of course we would believe in him! Why wouldn't we? So it must be his fault in hiding away from us. It's like he's playing mind games with us – expecting us to figure it all out.

The words in our text are spoken by a friend of Job called Zophar. You know the story of Job? How he lost everything – his wealth, his family, his status and his health – and now his friend is telling him not to question God – how can you figure it out? Job understandably does not appreciate friends who keep twisting his words and trying to say that he really must be to blame. 'Job, you are suffering because you must have sinned.

Job, do you think that by searching you can find God?' But Job reacts by saying, 'Don't you think that I know God is beyond finding out? I know that!'

'To God belong wisdom and power; counsel and understanding are his' (Job 12:13).

The trouble is, can we know God? Is he too far beyond us? Is he what the theologians call so 'transcendent' that we cannot find him or know him? That is certainly what Muslim theology teaches. Allah is unknowable.

The atheist philosopher Bertrand Russell was once asked what would he say if he died and appeared before the God he did not believe in? He replied, 'Sir, why did you take such pains to hide yourself?'[6]

Friedrich Nietzsche likewise stated, 'It is a duty of God to be truthful towards mankind and clear in the manner of his communications.'[7] These might seem clear and obvious statements, but there is one major flaw in them. Can you spot it?

What if God has made himself clear? What if, instead of hiding, he has revealed himself? What if the problem is with us, not him? In question 8, we saw that God has clearly revealed himself in what he has made – his eternal power and divine nature have been clearly seen. Hebrews 1:1-3 says,

'In the past God spoke to our ancestors through the prophets at many times and in various ways, but in these last days he has spoken to us by his Son, whom he appointed heir of all things, and through whom also he made the universe. The Son is the radiance of God's glory and the exact representation of his being, sustaining all things by his powerful word.'

---

6. *These Things Must Happen*, Dave Gaffney, Tate Publishing, 2011.
7. Attributed to Friedrich Nietzsche, 1844-1900.

So God has shown himself. First of all in what he has made. Then he has 'set eternity in the human heart' (Ecclesiastes 3:11), so we have an awareness of him. Then, over hundreds of years, he sent his prophets to give us his Word. Finally, as the last revelation of himself, he sent his Son, Jesus who is 'the exact representation of his being'. Ah – but you say, that is no use to me because Jesus has gone and I can't find him. Except that Jesus sent the Spirit, and the Holy Spirit inspired the apostles to write the rest of the Bible and make it crystal clear who God is and what he wants. Even more than that, the Spirit works in our hearts and gives us the light of the knowledge of Christ.

We are without excuse. Even if we 'just' had the creation we would be without excuse. But we have so much more.

Jesus often said about his teaching, 'If you've got ears, then listen!' Everyone Jesus spoke to had ears, so what did he mean by this saying? He is asking if they have ears to hear, and are they prepared to listen? God has made himself clear ... so maybe the problem lies elsewhere? Maybe the problem is not with God being unclear, but us not being willing to open our eyes and see, or open our ears and hear, or open our minds and understand.

Let's think about it another way. Maybe it's God who is doing the searching? Maybe it's Jesus who came to seek and save the lost? That is the beautiful picture being presented in the gospel. The Son of Man came to seek and to save that which was lost. We seek him, because he is seeking us.

CONSIDER: How do you think that God could show himself more clearly? What obstacles get in the way of our seeing, hearing and understanding?

RECOMMENDED FURTHER READING:

Crazy Love – Francis Chan

PRAYER: Father God, you promise that those who seek you will find you. Lord, I want to know you. Surely you have put this desire in my heart? Show me your ways, LORD, teach me your paths, and lead me in the everlasting way. Let me know Jesus. For to know him, is to know you. In his name. Amen.

10. THE UNCREATED GOD

QUESTION: How did God come into existence? If God created the universe and everything in it, who created God?

BIBLE READING: Isaiah 40:21-31

TEXT: Do you not know?
Have you not heard?
The LORD is the everlasting God,
the Creator of the ends of the earth.
He will not grow tired or weary,
and his understanding no one can fathom
(Isaiah 40:28).

This is one of the most frequent and one of the most misunderstood questions I am ever asked. It is also very difficult to answer because it doesn't make sense – even when it is asked by very intelligent people like the famous atheist,

Richard Dawkins! Let me explain. It's like asking, 'Why can God not make a square circle?'

A square circle does not and cannot exist. Likewise an Almighty God, who created everything but is himself created, cannot exist. He could not be Almighty because the one who created him would be the Almighty one! Christians (and Jews and Muslims) do not believe in a 'created God'.

The answer to the question who made God, is simply – 'nobody'. God is not made. God is the Creator, not the creation. God is outside of time and space. (This is not to say that he is not also in time and space and that there is not plenty evidence for him there.) God creates *ex nihilo* (out of nothing). That's what makes him God. He does not craft from what is already there. He creates time, space and matter from nothing.

Who says that everything, including God himself, has to come from something? Christians and other theists do not argue that God was created. That is precisely the point. He did not come from anywhere. He has always been. He did not evolve, nor was he made. If there is a personal Creator of the Universe then it makes perfect sense to regard him as complex, beyond our understanding and eternal. We do not believe in a created God. We believe in an uncreated supernatural power.

These are the only possibilities for when we come to consider why anything exists at all.

SOMETHING CAME FROM NOTHING. At one point there was no universe, there was no material, there was no matter, no time, no space. And out of that big nothing there came the Big Bang and our vast universe, tiny planet, evolution and the human species. Such a notion is beyond the realms of reason and is a total nonsensical fantasy.

SOMETHING WAS ETERNAL. In other words, matter has always existed. There is a lump of rock, or a mass of gas or some kind of matter that had no beginning and will probably have no end. And at some point that matter exploded and we ended up with the finely tuned and wonderful universe we now inhabit.

SOMETHING WAS CREATED – EX NIHILO – OUT OF NOTHING. And that Creator has to be incredibly powerful, intelligent and awesome beyond our imagination.

This is what our passage in Isaiah teaches. God is the Everlasting God. The Creator of the ends of the earth. He is not created. He creates. Little wonder that we bow down in worship. We are the created. He is the Creator. It is so, so important that you do not think of God as some kind of super human. He is beyond our understanding.

But what about Jesus? Was he not created? In one of the most sublime, deep and profound things ever written (John 1), the apostle John tells us:

'In the beginning was the Word, and the Word was with God, and the Word was God. He was with God in the beginning. Through him all things were made; without him nothing was made that has been made (John 1:1-3).'

This is so marvellous. If God were 'just' the Creator, he could be distant and far from us – unknowable. But he sent his Son, Jesus (God is Father, Son and Spirit – something we will look at later) to reveal himself to us. Jesus is the Word. Jesus is God. Jesus is the Creator as well – without him nothing was made that has been made.

So not only do we not believe in a created God, we don't believe in a created Jesus. He is the eternal Word. He is from everlasting to everlasting.

'Yesterday, today forever, Jesus is the same.
All may change but Jesus, never. Glory to his name!'[8]

CONSIDER: Why do people find it so difficult to accept that God is uncreated? What should be the reaction of the created to the Creator?

RECOMMENDED FURTHER READING:
The Dawkins Letters – David Robertson

PRAYER: Almighty God, Creator of heaven and earth. You are the everlasting one. You alone are uncreated. We bow before you as your creatures. We worship you that you have made us in your image – that we can love, think and do good. O Lord, we grow tired and weary, we are so limited in our understanding and we are so sinful. Grant us your strength, your mind and your holiness. For your glory. Amen.

---

8. *Oh, how sweet the glorious message*, Albert B Simpson, 1890.

11. THE GENDER OF GOD

QUESTION: What Gender is God?

BIBLE READING: Numbers 23:1-26

TEXT: God is not human, that he should lie, not a human being, that he should change his mind. Does he speak and then not act? Does he promise and not fulfil? (Numbers 23:19).

You may have noticed that there is a great deal of confusion about what gender is today. The notion that human gender consisted of male and female, which was based upon biological, social and cultural differences, is now being replaced (at least in the influential areas of our society) with the view that gender is *just* a social construct (i.e. something made up by society), and that there can be many more genders.

What does the Bible say? It clearly teaches that human beings are made male and female.

'*So God created mankind in his own image, in the image of God he created them; male and female he created them*' (Genesis 1:27).

But notice that this verse also tells us that all human beings, male and female, are made in the image of God. So does this mean that God is both male and female? It can get very confusing. Consider the following:

The language used for God in the Bible is that of a male. It is God the Father. God is not 'it', he is a he! In an age when we are told to respect the pronouns that people wish to be used, perhaps it would be a good idea for us to use the personal pronouns that God has revealed himself with? It's not good for us to change the language we use about God to suit our culture or the fashions of the day. If we do so, we will soon end up creating not just language, but a God in our own image.

But that does not mean that God is male. Why not? One reason is that sometimes in the Bible female analogies and language are used of God. For example in Isaiah 66:13, God is spoken of as a mother.

'*As a mother comforts her child, so will I comfort you; and you will be comforted over Jerusalem*'.

But the main reason is that male and female are terms that are used for human beings – not for God. Despite all the caricatures, God is not some kind of superhuman or old man up in the sky. This is, of course, hard for us to understand and so our temptation is always to try and create a god in our own image. But the Bible gives us a different picture. One of the great Confessions of the Christian Church puts it this way, 'There is but one only living and true God, who is infinite in being and perfection, a most pure spirit, invisible, without body, parts, or passions' (*The Westminster Confession of Faith*).

Without body, parts or passions ... in other words the things that make gender. So in that sense, God is genderless.

We also need to beware of the heresy of teaching that the Trinity is like a human family – God the Father, the Holy Spirit the mother and Jesus the son. That is to read back into the Bible a twenty-first century concept of the family and again create a God in our own image. The Holy Spirit is not an 'it', nor a 'she'. When Jesus speaks of the Spirit he uses the male pronoun.

In all of this, it is important that we recognise two things. Firstly, it is hard for us, if not impossible for us, to conceive of God adequately. We need him to reveal himself to us. And he has done that in the Bible. So it is always best for us to stick with the 'revelation' that God has given us of himself.

Secondly, we understand God as he is revealed in Jesus. Hebrews 1 tells us that it is Jesus who is the exact representation of God's being. When we look at Jesus we see what God is like. Jesus came as a male human being, but his incarnation (God becoming flesh) is for all of us.

Perhaps sometimes we over-emphasise the differences between men and women – as though we are from different planets. We are all made in the image of God. Not in terms of gender, but we are logical beings, we are moral beings and we are holy beings. I wouldn't worry too much about the gender of God – to do so is to misunderstand who he is. The more important thing is to know God through Christ, and thus enable all of us, whatever our gender, to be better and renewed human beings.

CONSIDER: Why is it important to keep with the language of the Bible? What are the dangers with seeking to change the Bible so that it fits our culture? What are the practical implications of knowing that all men and all women are made in the image of God?

RECOMMENDED FURTHER READING:

Knowing God – J. I. Packer

PRAYER: O Lord our God, we bless you that you have revealed yourself to us through your name. We bless you that you are Father, Son and Holy Spirit. We thank you that all human beings, male or female are made in your image. Help us to know you are our Creator and Saviour. Amen.

12. THE TRINITY

QUESTION: I don't get the Trinity – do we kind of believe in three gods?

BIBLE READING: Matthew 28

TEXT: Then Jesus came to them and said, 'All authority in heaven and on earth has been given to me. Therefore go and make disciples of all nations, baptising them in the name of the Father and of the Son and of the Holy Spirit, and teaching them to obey everything I have commanded you. And surely I am with you always, to the very end of the age' (Matthew 28:18-20).

I have a copy of the *Shema Yisreal* on my desk – it is a Jewish prayer based upon Deuteronomy 6:4:

'Hear, O Israel: The LORD our God, the LORD is one.'

The belief in one God (monotheism) is central to the great monotheistic religions (Judaism, Christianity and Islam). Many other religions are polytheistic – they believe in many gods. By definition however there can only be one Almighty, all knowing, all-powerful creator, who made everything.

So Christians believe that there is one God. But we also believe in what is called the Trinity. This is a Latin term that is not found in the Bible. However, what it teaches is: there is one God, who exists in three persons, the Father, the Son and the Holy Spirit. Don't worry if you don't instantly grasp what that means – very clever theologians (and some not so clever!) have been wrestling with that for centuries. We are going to try and think about this, but please don't be surprised if you think 'this is way beyond me ...' It is way beyond all of us. However, just because we can't grasp it all, doesn't mean we shouldn't believe what God has told us about himself.

It's maybe best for us just to say what the Bible actually says. The Father is God (Philippians 1:2 talks of 'God our Father' as do many other parts of the Bible). The Son is God (Titus 2:13 speaks of Jesus as 'our great God and Saviour'). The Holy Spirit is God (Acts 5:3-4 talks about lying to the Spirit as being lying to God).

The Bible does not say that talking about the Father, the Son and the Holy Spirit are just different ways of talking about the same person. They are each spoken of as distinct persons. The Father sends the Son. He is not the Son. The Holy Spirit is sent by both the Father and the Son. He is not the Father and the Son. Jesus is God but he is not the Father or the Spirit. The Spirit is God, but he is not the Father or the Son. The Father is God, but he is not the Son or the Spirit.

Are you still with me? Let's go a little deeper. God has always been trinity. The Father did not become the Son; the Son did not become the Spirit. God has always been three in one.

The Trinity does not mean that God is divided into three different bits. The Father, the Son and the Spirit are each fully God. Colossians 2:9, for example, talks about 'all the fullness of the deity dwelling in bodily form' in Jesus. The Godness of God is in all three persons.

So, thus far we have the Bible teaching that the Father, the Son and the Spirit are distinct persons; that each is fully God; that there is only one God; and all three persons are the same God. There is one God who exists as three distinct persons.

Our verse for this study teaches all of those things. What we call the great commission tells us that there are three persons, (the Father, the Son and the Spirit), that they are all God, and that although they are distinct, yet we are baptised into the one name – which means that they share the same essence.

Here is where we run up against the problem of language. St Augustine argued that we speak, only in order not to be silent! We are trying to express in our limited language, the inexpressible God.

This is the basic understanding of the Trinity – God is one in essence, but three in person. This is not a contradiction because essence and person are different. What does essence mean? It's what you are. But God is not made of 'stuff' – he is spirit. So we are saying that this applies to the three persons. What do we mean by person? – not a distinct individual – like you and I as humans can exist apart from one another. Person in this sense means personal, in that there is an 'I' and a 'you'. Essence is what you are, person is who you are.

Okay. I'm going to stop there, because that is more than enough! But let me leave you with this thought. Because God is Trinity he is love. The Father, the Son and the Spirit are love. The great news is that they invite us to share in that love.

CONSIDER: Do you think we should be able to understand God? Why is the Trinity important? Does it matter that Jesus is God and man?

RECOMMENDED FURTHER READING:

Delighting in the Trinity – Michael Reeves

PRAYER: Lord God, Father, Son and Holy Spirit. You are far beyond our understanding, but we bless and thank you that you have revealed yourself to us. You are our Father – the one who loves and gives. You are the Son, the one who died for us and is risen for us. You are the Spirit, the one who fills us and changes us. Triune God, we bow before you and cry, 'Holy, Holy, Holy, is the Lord God Almighty.'

13. THE MIND OF GOD

BIBLE READING: 1 Corinthians 2:6-16

TEXT: ... 'Who has known the mind of the Lord so as to instruct him?' But we have the mind of Christ (1 Corinthians 2:16).

Why does it matter what God thinks? This is the type of question that shows that the questioner is not really thinking, or does not really know what they are asking. It's good that God is patient with us!

Imagine that you are going for an interview to get a job and you bump into someone who gives you an angry comment and asks you to watch where you are going. You turn to your friends and say, 'Who does that guy think he is? Why should I care what he thinks?' You then head into the interview room and the person you have just mocked is sitting behind the interview desk – he is the head of the company and the person who will decide whether to employ you or not. Suddenly it really does matter what he thinks!

When we ask the question, 'Why does it matter what God thinks?', it shows that we are not really aware of who God is, or indeed who we are. He is the Almighty God. He is our Creator. He is our Judge. One day we will have to stand before him and give account of everything we have done with all the good gifts he has given us – including the gift of our own life.

We will also have to give account for every wrong action done, every cruel word spoken and every careless thought. In other words, it matters what our minds think about God, because his mind is infinitely greater and one day we will have to answer to him.

But it's not just that one day we will have to answer on the day of judgement. It matters what God thinks because we need guidance and hope for today. Paul tells the Corinthians that the rulers of this age did not understand who Jesus was or what God was doing through Jesus and so they crucified the Lord of glory. But God intended even that most evil of deeds for good.

'What no eye has seen, what no ear has heard, and what no human mind has conceived – the things that God has prepared for those who love him' (1 Corinthians 2:9).

You and I will often dream and think about the good things that we have planned for our lives. Perhaps you would like to get married, or become rich, or become famous, or have children, or play for Barcelona (or Real Madrid!)? Here is the incredible thing – however great your thoughts and dreams, you can never out-think and out-dream what God has planned for you! That's why it's so important to know the mind of God, because it is so beautiful and good and pure – unlike any human mind.

'For I know the plans I have for you,' declares the LORD, 'plans to prosper you and not to harm you, plans to give you hope and a future' (Jeremiah 29:11).

'How precious to me are your thoughts, God! How vast is the sum of them!' (Psalm 139:17).

This is another wonderful thing. There is always more to learn. There is always deeper to go. God does not reveal everything to us all at once. God's thoughts are like the drops of water in the ocean. They are too numerous to count and beyond compare. We will bathe in them for all eternity!

The question then arises: how do we know what God's thoughts are? Paul answers. They are revealed to us by his Spirit. No one knows the thoughts of God except the Spirit of God. He teaches us, not in words that come from human teachers, but in words taught by the Spirit. That is why it is so important to realise that the Bible is not just something made up by human beings – it is the very words of God, given to us to reveal the mind of God. When we have the Spirit of God, we accept his words and we are able to know the mind of Christ. As Paul tells us in Romans 12:2:

'Do not conform to the pattern of this world, but be transformed by the renewing of your mind. Then you will be able to test and approve what God's will is—his good, pleasing and perfect will.'

He tells the Philippians 'to have the mind of Christ' (Philippians 2:5). Isn't it an absolutely incredible thing – not only that we can know what God thinks, but also as we grow and develop as Christians, that we can have the mind of Christ?

The great scientist Stephen Hawking asked the question: What is the purpose of the universe? He answered by saying:

'If we find the answer to that, it would be the ultimate triumph of human reason – for then we would know the mind of God'.[9]

I think he really meant that we would become God. How sad that as an atheist he did not grasp that we do know the mind of God, not by human reason, but by God's revelation. God has told us what the purpose of the universe is – to glorify him and declare his praises. And to provide a home for us – the creatures he made in his own image! We have the mind of Christ.

CONSIDER: Once you know who God is, once you realise how your finite mind cannot comprehend the infinite mind of God, once you know that he is good and beautiful and love, then you will never ask why it is important to know the mind of God. The question won't make any sense to you. Knowing Christ is everything.

RECOMMENDED FURTHER READING:
Discovering God's Will – Sinclair B. Ferguson

PRAYER: O Lord God, you are beyond searching and yet you have created us with minds that do search. We bless you that you do not leave us to guess, but that in your mercy, through your Spirit and Son, you have revealed your will and your glory to us. O Lord, give us the mind of Christ. Amen.

---

9. Ibid.

14. GOD AND SUFFERING

QUESTION: Why did God kill my father and we suffered because we became orphans? If God is all good and almighty, why do we observe earthquakes and babies diagnosed with terminal illnesses? Why do bad things happen if God wants the best for us?

BIBLE READING: Psalm 119:65-72

TEXT: You are good and you do what is good; teach me your decrees (Psalm 119:68).

In the previous chapter we talked about God's thoughts and plans being good for us. That immediately raises the questions we now face in this chapter – which some people think are the most difficult questions of all. If God is good then why do bad things happen? If God created the world good, how come there are bad things like diseases? Surely if God is all-powerful he would be able to prevent bad things happening? If he is good he would want to prevent bad things happening? So if bad things happen then it either means that God is not all-powerful or he is not good?

At one level this is a very powerful argument. So powerful in fact that it causes many people to turn away from belief in God. It's not surprising that it is one of the devil's favourite tricks to use. But remember, the devil is a liar. This is also something I have been thinking about for many years. When I was a young minister I went to collect a girl who was coming to our youth club in the church. I was met at the door by a very angry father who told me that he didn't believe in God and that he hated him anyway. Why? Because 'God killed my wife'. We talked for a while and I asked him, how did your wife die? Cancer. Why do you think God killed her? In the course of our discussion I pointed out that God did not kill his wife, although God did not heal her either, but are we really going to blame God for everything bad that happens in this world? I also told him that the most important thing is not *why* God allows bad things to happen, but what has God done, or will do about evil. This is a big, big question so let me just outline some things that may help. You can read more about this in a long talk I gave on the subject (the link is on page 66).

The Bible teaches that God is good (see our text). Indeed he is the only source of good and the very definition of good. He cannot even look upon evil, never mind do it.

The Bible also teaches that God is all-powerful. So how did evil come to exist? Did a good God create evil? Was he powerless to prevent it?

A North African man called Augustine thought about this over 1,500 years ago and came up with what I think is a brilliant biblical answer. Let me summarise it in this way.

- God created all things.
- Evil is not a created thing – it is the absence of good.
- God did not create evil, but permits it for the good.

'And, in the universe, even that which is called evil, when it is regulated and put in its own place, only enhances our admiration of the good; for we enjoy and value the good more when we compare it with the evil. For the Almighty God, who, as even the heathen acknowledge, has supreme power over all things, being Himself supremely good, would never permit the existence of anything evil among His works, if he were not so omnipotent and good that he can bring good even out of evil' (Enchiridion ch. 11).

God is so powerful that he can even bring good out of evil. God created the world with human beings in it and gave us a choice – to follow and love him freely or to choose evil. We chose evil. We chose to try and be gods ourselves. As a result, sin, death and evil entered God's good and perfect creation. They are now part of the natural order.

But God did not destroy the world, nor did he leave us to destroy ourselves. There are two ways God could deal with evil – one is to destroy us all now and throw us all into the fiery pit designed for the devil and his angels. The other is to send his Son to die for our sins and so defeat death, sin and the devil. As we will see in the next chapter this is what he did!

So to answer the questions above. God did not kill your father and God does love the widows and orphans – he is a Father to the fatherless. Because humanity turned away from God, we live in a fallen and broken world where bad things do happen. But we can pray 'deliver us from evil.' God does want the best for us and is so great and powerful that he can make the bad things turn out for the best.

'And we know that in all things God works for the good of those who love him, who have been called according to his purpose' (Romans 8:28).

CONSIDER: How would you help someone who is suffering? What did Jesus do to save us from suffering? Do you trust God to bring good, even out of what appears evil to us?

RECOMMENDED FURTHER READING:
http://www.clayton.tv/new/0i0/1187/
https://theweeflea.com/2014/07/21/the-apologetic-of-evil-1/
Walking with God Through Pain and Suffering - Tim Keller

PRAYER: Lord, you are good and the giver of all things good. I trust your commands. I trust your Word. I trust your goodness. It was good for me to be afflicted so that I might learn your decrees. Your Word is more precious to me than anything in the world. In the midst of all my pain, help me to know that you are good. Deliver us from evil. In Jesus' name, Amen.

15. THE DEATH OF JESUS

QUESTION: Why did God let Jesus die, when he could have saved him? If God is Almighty why doesn't he beat the devil?

BIBLE READING: John 3:14-21

TEXT: For God so loved the world that he gave his one and only Son, that whoever believes in him shall not perish but have eternal life (John 3:16).

God's response to the big question of suffering – is to give us an even bigger answer! One that will blow your mind. One that even the angels are amazed at. One that will cause you to worship Jesus for all eternity.

When Paul wrote to the Romans he explained the cross: why it was necessary, what happened and what the results were. In Romans 5:6-8, he says:

'You see, at just the right time, when we were still powerless, Christ died for the ungodly. Very rarely will anyone die for a righteous person, though for a good person someone might possibly dare to die. But God demonstrates his own love for us in this: While we were still sinners, Christ died for us.'

We talk about people giving their lives for others, but that is very rare. We may give our lives for those we love and those who love us. But Paul tells us – Jesus died for his enemies – for those who hated him. The danger is that we say or sing this so often in church that we forget how astonishing it is. Even more when we think about it from the Father's perspective. *God so loved the world that he gave his one and only Son.* I have a son and I love him to bits (as well as my two daughters). I could conceive of dying for them. I cannot conceive any circumstances in which I would give the life of my son for anyone – let alone those who hate me! Yet this is what God did.

God let Jesus die because he loved us and wanted to save us. How does the death of Jesus do that? Every one of our sins is a sin against a holy God, which deserves his eternal punishment. God is a just God and he cannot simply allow evil and sin to go unpunished. But he is a loving God and so, instead of punishing his people with hell, he sends his Son to suffer our hell for us. So in one moment on earth, the eternal Son of God takes upon himself all our sin and receives the eternal punishment due to us. This is why God let Jesus die. It's why Jesus agreed to go to the cross. It's why he prayed in the garden of Gethsemane:

'Father, if you are willing, take this cup from me; yet not my will, but yours be done' (Luke 22:42).

It's why the Holy Spirit did not intervene with ten thousand angels to rescue Jesus. God let Jesus die on the cross because he loved you and me. Jesus died on the cross because he loved us. Never ever let the wonder of that truth turn into cliché or boredom for you. There is no greater truth in the world.

'... The life I live in the body I live by faith in the Son of God, who loved me and gave himself for me' (Galatians 2:20).

As for the second part of the question – why doesn't God just beat the devil? He did – through the cross. God could have defeated the devil by sending him straight to hell. But if he had done so, we would have gone with him because God would also have to punish the evil within us. So how could God remain just and yet justify (save/make right) those who were his enemies? The answer is through the cross. It is the cross that defeats the devil. That's why Jesus said before he went to the cross, *'I saw Satan fall like lightning from heaven'* (Luke 10:18).

Satan thought that by killing the Son of God he had won. Instead it was the means of his defeat. '

And having disarmed the powers and authorities, he made a public spectacle of them, triumphing over them by the cross' (Colossians 2:15).

C.S. Lewis wrote about this in *The Lion, the Witch and the Wardrobe* – where the White Witch (and all her and Aslan's followers) thought that she had won when Aslan laid down his life for Edmund. But there was a deeper power at work ... a deeper law. That is exactly what happened at the cross. Satan is defeated, we are saved and God is glorified.

CONSIDER: Do you understand that cross? What does it tell you about our sin that they needed the death of the pure Son of God to forgive them? What does it tell you about the love of God?

RECOMMENDED FURTHER READING:
The Cross of Christ – John Stott
The Lion, the Witch and the Wardrobe – C.S. Lewis

PRAYER: Lord, the cross is a mystery. It is horrible and ugly. It is foolish. It is offensive. And yet it is by the foolishness and offensiveness of the cross that we are saved. So for us, it is beautiful. Father, we bless you that you gave your Son. Jesus, we bless you that you laid down your life for us willingly. Holy Spirit, we ask that you would help us to feel, understand and know the wonder of the cross, in the name of the Father, the Son and the Holy Spirit. Amen.

16. JESUS - THE ONLY SAVIOUR

QUESTION: Why do Christians believe that Jesus is the only Saviour? Why not someone else?

BIBLE READING: Acts 4:1-12

TEXT: Salvation is found in no one else, for there is no other name under heaven given to mankind by which we must be saved (Acts 4:12).

To some modern ears it appears a bit arrogant to claim that our way is the only way. I guess that is partly what lies behind this question. It does at first glance sound like we are saying, 'we are right and everyone else is wrong!' And it does sound a lot more reasonable and nice to say that, whilst there is one God, there are many ways to that God, of which Jesus is only one.

It sounds nice. But if you stop to think about it, it doesn't make much sense. Suppose you come to visit my city (Dundee in Scotland), and you don't really know the area but you want to go and visit the lovely wee town of St Andrews, just fifteen miles away. You go into the city centre and you ask a group standing there, 'How do I get to St Andrews?' One man says that you need to head up the road to Aberdeen and you will get there. Another says, 'You need to take the road to Perth and keep heading West.' A woman interrupts and declares, 'Get in a boat at the harbour and go to Norway.' Whilst another says, 'Head due north over the mountains and you will get to St Andrews.' Finally a small girl says, 'No, you need to go over the Tay Bridge and then turn left and soon you will come to St Andrews.' The others all turn on her and shout, 'How dare you be so arrogant! What makes you think that there is only one way?! And why do you think your way is the right way?' The answer of course is because it is!

And it's exactly the same with Jesus. He is the only way. There is no other name under heaven given to all humanity by which we must be saved. Why is that the case? Well, consider the following questions:

Who else is perfect? There is none good – no not one. Except Jesus Christ. No sin was ever found in him.

Who else spoke such truth and such beauty? When people heard him speak they were amazed because he spoke as someone who had authority and who knew what he was talking about – unlike the religious teachers who spoke about God from their limited knowledge – he came from the heart of the Trinity and told us what he had heard. They at best, spoke about God. He spoke the words of God.

Who else is going to die for you? Most of the religious leaders in the world expect people to die for them, but Jesus died for his people.

Who else is the Son of God? Who else is the source of light, life and love? Who else did the Father give?

The 'name' is important here. Because every time God reveals his name in the Bible it tells us something about him. He is Yahweh (I AM who I AM, the eternal one). He is Jehovah Jireh (God my provider). He is the Lord. He is the Shepherd. The name of Jesus means 'Saviour'. He is the Saviour. He is the only Saviour. Mohammed, Buddha, David, Paul, Mary, or any of the thousands of people or supposed gods cannot save us. Only Christ can. Salvation is found in no one else. It is at the name of Jesus that every knee will bow.

In the early church, the Christians who were being persecuted had a special sign – the sign of the fish. The Greek word for fish is 'ichthus'. The Christians took the first letters of the words in this phrase – *Iēsous Christos Theou Yios Sōtēr*', (Translated it means Jesus Christ, Son of God, Saviour) to spell ichthus. Jesus Christ is the Son of God. He is the only Saviour.

This is the opposite of arrogant. Because Jesus is the Saviour for the whole world he is not the God of one culture or one way of life. He is the Saviour of the world. Peter and the disciples were told by the rulers, elders and teachers of the law in Jerusalem, not to speak anymore about this 'name'. But their response was brilliant and should be ours:

'We cannot help speaking about what we have seen and heard' (Acts 4:20).

There is a Saviour and his name is Jesus.

CONSIDER: Why is it not arrogant to say that Jesus is the only way? What is different about Jesus compared with every other supposed saviour?

RECOMMENDED FURTHER READING:
Magnificent Obsession – David Robertson

PRAYER: Lord Jesus Christ, you are the Saviour. You are our only Saviour. You loved us and gave yourself for us. To whom else can we go? You have the words of life! Please reveal yourself more and more to us. We want to know you more, because to know you is to love you. We ask it for our good and your glory. Amen.

17. FORGIVENESS

QUESTION: How do you achieve forgiveness?

BIBLE READING: Hebrews 9:11-28

TEXT: In fact, the law requires that nearly everything be cleansed with blood, and without the shedding of blood there is no forgiveness.... Just as people are destined to die once, and after that to face judgement, so Christ was sacrificed once to take away the sins of many; and he will appear a second time, not to bear sin, but to bring salvation to those who are waiting for him (Hebrews 9:22 and 27-28).

The answer to the question of how you achieve forgiveness is very simple. You don't. You can't. It is impossible for anyone to 'achieve' forgiveness. When we do something wrong against a friend or someone in our family, I guess we can make up for it – we can atone for it. I once kicked a ball through a window and I atoned for it by paying for the glass to be replaced. But when we sin against a pure and holy God, it's not just a small matter and it's nothing we can atone for.

There are some people who are conscious they have done something really wrong and they spend the whole of their life trying to make atonement. They never can. And none of us can make atonement for our sin against God (because although sins are also against others, and even ourselves, ultimately they are against God).

But won't religion work? No. It never does. You can go to church, read the Bible, do the rosary, say your prayers and none of that can forgive you. In the Old Testament God gave the people a sacrificial system (described in great detail in the book of Leviticus) but, as the writer to the Hebrews reminds us, the blood of bulls and goats can never take away sin. They provide outward cleansing, a ritual cleansing, but they cannot deal with the heart of the matter – which is our heart. That's not just true of the Old Testament church, it's also true of the New Testament church. When people think that they can just perform a religious ritual and then they will be forgiven – they do not grasp the depth and horror of their own sin. Religion can't forgive anyone.

What about good deeds? If we have done some bad things can we not balance it out by doing some good deeds so at the end God will say – well done you, I forgive you for the bad things you have done because of the good things you have done!? Thinking like that means that we don't appreciate the hellishness and power of sin, nor our own inability to do any saving good. There is none good. No, not one.

So if we can't achieve forgiveness does that just mean we have to grin and bear it? Do we just have to suppress our guilt, or pretend it's not there, or just try to hide it? No. As the psalmist tells us, *'there is forgiveness with you, that we may with reverence serve you'* (Psalm 130:4). Will God just forgive us because as the French philosopher Rousseau said, 'C'est son métier'[10] (that's his job)? Again no. God is a faithful and just God. He cannot just forgive. Sin must be dealt with.

When I was a young Christian I woke up one morning and felt just so depressed at my own sin that I did not want to read the Bible and thought I could do nothing. But I forced myself to open it. My reading for the day was Isaiah 6. I have never forgotten these words – they were so directly appropriate for me (incidentally let me encourage you to read the Bible systematically every day – you will be astonished at how many times in your life that the Word of the Lord for that day is just what you needed – it's almost as if God intended it that way!).

When Isaiah saw the holiness and glory of God he cried out:

'Woe to me! ... I am ruined! For I am a man of unclean lips, and I live among a people of unclean lips, and my eyes have seen the King, the LORD Almighty' (Isaiah 6:5).

He thought he was finished. But then an angel flew to him with a live coal from the altar.

'With it he touched my mouth and said, "See, this has touched your lips; your guilt is taken away and your sin is atoned for"' (Isaiah 6:7).

What great words! What a great truth! Your guilt is taken away and your sin is atoned for!

I can't 'achieve' forgiveness. Christ has achieved forgiveness. His death on the cross is what forgives us. It's not the blood of bulls and goats. It's the blood of Christ. We are not clothed in our good works, but we are clothed with the righteousness of Christ. All of us who come to him are forgiven. You don't achieve forgiveness; you come to the one who can forgive. The words of the old hymn are helpful:

---

10. Jean-Jacques Rousseau, French philosopher, 1712-1778.

Just as I am, without one plea,
But that Thy blood was shed for me,
And that Thou bid'st me come to Thee,
O Lamb of God, I come! I come!

Just as I am, and waiting not
To rid my soul of one dark blot;
To Thee whose blood can cleanse each spot,
O Lamb of God, I come, I come![11]

CONSIDER: How do we get rid of guilt? Can guilt ever be a good thing? If Christ forgives us all our sin does that give us an excuse to go on sinning?

RECOMMENDED FURTHER READING:
Assurance – Overcoming the Difficulty of Knowing Forgiveness – John Owen

PRAYER:
Rock of Ages, cleft for me, let me hide myself in Thee;
Let the water and the blood, from Thy wounded side which flowed, be of sin the double cure,
Save from wrath and make me pure.

Not the labour of my hands, can fulfil Thy law's demands;
Could my zeal no respite know, could my tears forever flow,
All for sin could not atone; thou must save, and Thou alone.

Nothing in my hand I bring, simply to Thy cross I cling;
Naked, come to Thee for dress; helpless, look to Thee for grace; Foul, I to the fountain fly; wash me, Saviour, or I die.[12]

---

11. *Just as I am,* Charlotte Elliot 1789-1871, published 1835.
12. *Rock of Ages,* Augustus M. Toplady, 1740-1778, published 1763.

18. HELL

QUESTION: If we are only here for a short time how do we deserve eternal punishment?

BIBLE READING: Isaiah 30:8-18

TEXT: Yet the LORD longs to be gracious to you;
therefore he will rise up to show you compassion.
For the LORD is a God of justice.
Blessed are all who wait for him! (Isaiah 30:18)

The teaching about hell is so hard. It's hard to take in, hard to grasp, hard to preach and hard to ignore. This is not a teaching that comes primarily from the Old Testament, or from Paul, Peter or John. The person who teaches most about hell, is the loving, gentle and compassionate Jesus. The only reason I believe in hell is because Jesus does – and I follow Jesus.

C.S. Lewis summarises the position really well: *'There is no doctrine which I would more willingly remove from Christianity than this, if it lay in my power. But it has the full support of Scripture and, specially, of our Lord's own words; it has always been held by*

Christendom; and it has the support of reason.'[13] But as with all things we need to be really careful that we neither take away nor add to the Bible. There are different views that Christians have about hell. Some think that there is no hell. Others that whilst it exists no one but the devil goes there. They believe that either everyone is saved or that those who don't go to heaven cease to exist. Others believe that people go to hell, but that whilst hell is eternal, the punishment is not. The traditional view in the Christian church is that hell is eternal and that the punishment is eternal. So what does Jesus say?

It is very difficult to claim to be a follower of the Jesus of the Bible and then turn round and say that either hell doesn't exist, or that no one goes there. Jesus says: *'They will throw them into the blazing furnace, where there will be weeping and gnashing of teeth.'* (Matthew 13:42). He also tells us:

'Then he will say to those on his left, "Depart from me, you who are cursed, into the eternal fire prepared for the devil and his angels"' (Matthew 25:41).

You cannot claim to follow Jesus and his teachings if you believe that hell does not exist or that no one goes there. You can argue that the language is metaphorical if you wish – but it is still a horrible metaphor for something horrible. Jesus teaches that hell is a place of punishment and a place of outer darkness.

But is the punishment eternal? It is in that its consequences are eternal. But some Christians argue that the Bible does not teach that man has an immortal soul and that at some point God will end the punishment. Others believe that human beings continue to sin in hell, and hate God so that punishment is ongoing.

---

13. *The Problem of Pain*, C.S. Lewis, Collins, 2012.

I have often agonized about this. And I'm not sure I have easy answers. I think I want to go as far as the Bible goes and no further. Hell exists. Some people do go there. God is just and any punishment he gives will be absolutely just. All the evil in the universe will be confined to hell. That makes it a place that none of us should want to go to. One of the most sickening things I have ever seen is tens of thousands of people jumping up and down and singing along to ACDC's 'Highway to Hell'. They also sing that 'hell ain't a bad place to be'. Of course it's meant both as a joke and as bravado – but it ain't funny and it ain't brave. Hell is the most dreadful place to be, and none of us should rejoice at being on the highway there.

But let's come back to our text. It tells us that God is a God of justice (so you don't need to worry about unjust punishment in hell) and that he is a God of compassion who longs to be gracious to us. At the end of the day – those who go to hell are those who deserve to be there and who have chosen to be there. As C.S. Lewis argues in *The Great Divorce*, 'There are only two kinds of people in the end: those who say to God, *"Thy will be done,"* and those to whom God says, in the end, *"Thy will be done."*'[14]

CONSIDER: There is really one thing for you to consider here. Which road are you on? Have you accepted Jesus' great offer of salvation and eternal life, or are you on the Highway to Hell? Do you choose to live eternally with God or without him? 'Come to me,' says Jesus. Will you?

---

14. *The Great Divorce*, C.S. Lewis, Collins, 2012.

RECOMMENDED FURTHER READING:

God, That's Not Fair - Understanding Eternal Punishment and the Christian's Urgent Mission - Dick Dowsett
Crucial Questions about Hell - Ajith Fernando

PRAYER: O Lord, this is a hard teaching. Who can bear it? We do not know the depth and horror of our sin, so we cannot grasp the necessity and justice of hell. But we know that you are a gracious and compassionate God, as well as being a God of justice. So we simply pray – deliver us from evil. Deliver us from hell and enable us to be with you forever. Amen.

19. THE CERTAINTY OF HEAVEN

QUESTION: How can I know for sure where I will go when I die?

BIBLE READING: 1 John 5:11-21

TEXT: And this is the testimony: God has given us eternal life, and this life is in his Son. Whoever has the Son has life; whoever does not have the Son of God does not have life. I write these things to you who believe in the name of the Son of God so that you may know that you have eternal life (1 John 5:11-13).

This is such an important question. How can we know? If you followed most man-made religions you wouldn't know. Because most say that IF you are good enough you will get to paradise. But biblical Christianity is so different. Just look at what John tells us.

God gives us eternal life. How does he do that? It is in his Son. It is very simple. If you have the Son of God you have eternal life. If you don't have Jesus, you don't have eternal life. How can we know if we have the Son? If we believe in him and trust in him, then we have him. Believe is not just 'believe about' but rather trust in.

If you are trusting in yourself, your good works, your family, your friends or anything else then be assured you do not have, and you will not receive eternal life. If, however, you know that the only person who can save you is Jesus, and if you are trusting in him and what he has done on the cross – it's not that you *will* have eternal life – you *do* have eternal life.

But can we lose that eternal life? Some Christians think we can. They think that we must persevere to the end and that you can be a real Christian and lose your salvation so that you need to be born again, again! This is not what Jesus says:

'I give them eternal life, and they shall never perish; no one will snatch them out of my hand. My Father, who has given them to me, is greater than all no one can snatch them out of my Father's hand' (John 10:28-29).

We are in the hand of Jesus. We are in the Father's hand. And he won't let us go. Once you have eternal life it is forever ... that's the meaning of the word 'eternal'. This is a doctrine known as 'the perseverance of the saints'. It's not so much that we persevere (although we must), but rather that the Lord perseveres with us. The reason we do not give up on him, is that he does not give up on us.

There are passages in the Bible which seem to suggest that Christians can lose their salvation and which rightly warn us about turning away from the living God, but I think when you read them in the light of the whole of Scripture you can see that they are warning us not to take salvation lightly. Indeed, the ultimate sign that we are saved, is that we persevere. Without becoming too introspective it is very important for us to ask whether we really do believe and trust in Christ. Have we just had a 'religious' experience or have we really given ourselves wholly to Jesus? For example, when people say I believe in Jesus as my Saviour, but not as my Lord, they are indicating that they do not know Jesus as either Saviour or Lord. We can't have him as the one without the other.

Sometimes I have had doubts about a lot of things – not least my own heart and condition. All I am left with is this simple faith – I believe and trust in Jesus Christ as the Son of God, who loved me and gave himself for me. That may be faith as small as a mustard seed, but it is real and it can move mountains of doubt.

'We know also that the Son of God has come and has given us understanding, so that we may know him who is true. And we are in him who is true by being in his Son Jesus Christ. He is the true God and eternal life' (1 John 5:20).

If you are not yet a Christian – you need to seek Christ. You need to accept Christ. You need to give your whole life to Christ. When you do so – be assured – you have eternal life and no-one can snatch you out of his hand.

CONSIDER: How do we know we have eternal life? Have you given your life to Jesus? Are you trusting in something or someone else to save you? What do you do when you doubt these things?

RECOMMENDED FURTHER READING:
Assurance – J.C. Ryle - (this is a small booklet taken from his larger book – *Holiness* – well worth reading).

PRAYER: Lord Jesus, we thank you for your promises. We thank you that you do not lie and cannot lie. We thank you that you promised that whoever comes to you, you would never turn away and that whoever believes in you has eternal life. Lord, we believe, help our unbelief and give us the gift of faith in you. Amen.

20. ANIMALS IN HEAVEN

QUESTION: Do dogs go to heaven?

BIBLE READING: Psalm 104:24-35

TEXT: All creatures look to you
             to give them their food at the proper time.
             When you give it to them,
             they gather it up;
             when you open your hand,
             they are satisfied with good things.
             When you hide your face,
             they are terrified;
             when you take away their breath,
             they die and return to the dust.
             When you send your Spirit,
             they are created,
             and you renew the face of the ground
             (Psalm 104:27-30).

Many of us have close relationships with our animals. I grew up on a farm and loved being with the different animals. I had pet guinea pigs, rabbits and dogs. We had a black Labrador retriever called Tweed, and a wee Scottie dog called Scruff. When I became a minister we took a dog from a refuge. We named her Tess. It was very hard when Tess had to be put down, because she was a sheep worrier. Sometimes parents will tell their children when a favourite family pet dies, that Fido is in heaven. But this is not true. When our goldfish, who was called Speedy, was a little too speedy one day and launched herself out of the bowl with such force that she died – we may have held a wee burial, but there was no promise that Speedy was in heaven, 'in the sure and certain hope of the resurrection'. Goldfish are not resurrected. Humans are.

C.S. Lewis speculated in his book, *The Problem of Pain*,[15] that some animals might enter heaven through their relationship with humans. But there is no biblical warrant for that at all. We understand from the Bible that animals have animal life, but they do not have human spirits. Human beings who go to heaven are there when their spirits and resurrected bodies are re-united. Animals don't have spirits to reunite. I don't think that it is reasonable to argue that particular animals go to heaven. Our text tells us that when God takes away their breath, they die and return to dust.

Does that not happen to human beings? We certainly return to dust – dust we are and to dust we shall return. But we are more than dust.

---

15. Ibid.

'Then the LORD God formed a man from the dust of the ground and breathed into his nostrils the breath of life, and the man became a living being' (Genesis 2:7).

We have bodies and spirits. Animals don't. We are made in the image of God – animals are not. Being made in the image of God does not mean that God has a body like us – it means that we are personal beings, with knowledge, righteousness and holiness. We are moral beings. Animals are not. They die but they do not face judgement. We do.

However, that is not the same as saying that there will be no animals in heaven. I think there will. Why? Because it's a new heavens and a new earth. It's really a renewal of the whole creation and surely that includes animals? Paul tells us that the whole creation is waiting for the children of God to be revealed.

'For the creation waits in eager expectation for the children of God to be revealed. For the creation was subjected to frustration, not by its own choice, but by the will of the one who subjected it, in hope that the creation itself will be liberated from its bondage to decay and brought into the freedom and glory of the children of God' (Romans 8:19-21).

Although humans are different from animals, they too are God's creatures and we as the stewards of that creation, are to look after them and care for them. William Wilberforce is famous because he led the campaign that eventually led to the abolition of the slave trade. What many people do not know is that he was also the founder of the RSPCA (Royal Society for Prevention of Cruelty to Animals). That is to be the attitude of God's special creation, humanity, to all his creation – we are to care for it.

CONSIDER: How should Christians treat animals? What is the difference between animals and human beings?

RECOMMENDED FURTHER READING:
Creation Care: A Biblical Theology of the Natural World – Douglas Moo

PRAYER: Lord God, our Creator, we thank you for the variety of your creation. You have made many wondrous things. We thank you especially for the animals that are our pets and companions. Help us to treat them well. We look forward to being part of the new creation, the new heavens and the new earth. Fit us for that day, in your name. Amen.

21. SUICIDE

BIBLE READING: Judges 16:23-31

TEXT: Samson said, 'Let me die with the Philistines!' Then he pushed with all his might, and down came the temple on the rulers and all the people in it. Thus he killed many more when he died than while he lived' (Judges 16:30).

In December 1856, Hugh Miller, a church leader in Scotland, a man of science and a great author, got out of bed and wrote this message to his wife:

'My brain burns. I must have walked and a fearful dream rises upon me. I cannot bear the horrible thought. God and Father of the Lord Jesus Christ have mercy upon me. Dearest Lydia, dear children farewell. My brain burns as the recollection grows, my dear wife farewell. Hugh Miller.'

He then went and shot himself. To this day people have speculated as to why. He was clearly in great agony

- mentally and possibly physically. What happens to Christians who do that?

I don't need to go back to the nineteenth century, or to read about suicides in other countries, to know that this is still an issue today. In my years as a minister I have known several Christians who have committed suicide. The beautiful, intelligent young student who had everything going for her; the middle-aged family man; the minister whose life and ministry went horribly wrong. Even to think about these is heart-breaking.

Suicide is a dreadful thing. It may seem like a good solution to the person who is so depressed that they do not think life is worth living, but the problem is that they are not always thinking straight. Indeed in some cases they may not be thinking at all. They forget that they are usually leaving behind a people and a community who will be distraught and in despair at their death. It's a sin against the community. But they also forget that it is God alone who has the right to take someone's life. We do not normally have the right to take our own life. So yes – it is a sin. It is also a terrible testimony to the world. I recall one famous existentialist philosopher saying that he could not live consistently with his philosophy of despair because it would mean he would have to commit suicide. The trouble with a Christian who commits suicide is that it is inconsistent with our belief in the goodness, forgiveness and sovereignty of God.

But whilst we acknowledge that it is a sin against ourselves, the community and God, why would that mean we don't go to heaven? I wonder where this idea comes from? Is it a residue of a belief that those who die with unconfessed sin are not forgiven? Is it because it is considered a 'mortal' or unforgivable sin? That is certainly not what the Bible teaches.

In today's passage we read of a suicide in the Bible. Samson, by pulling down the temple of the pagans upon himself, did kill himself – as well as many of Israel's enemies. I suppose that is one example where suicide is at least understandable if not excused. Giving our lives for others might also be considered a good form of suicide.

But what about those who kill themselves out of despair or to get away from the fears, darkness, guilt and problems they face? Are they committing a sin that cannot be forgiven? We need to remember that Jesus died for all our sins, past, present and future. When we become Christians, Jesus doesn't say, 'That's fine. That's the slate wiped clean. Now you had better be sure you don't sin anymore because there is nothing more I can do for you.' If that were the case we would all be in deep trouble!

None of us are in the position where we can look back on the life of Hugh Miller and say, 'this is why he committed suicide'. We don't know. And when we don't know about such personal and deep matters, we have even more reason to keep silent. We cannot judge. All we must do is seek to help those who are left and try to understand and encourage those who are thinking of suicide to realise that their lives are worth living.

I don't think that the Christians I have known, who have committed suicide, are excluded from heaven. The blood of Jesus cleanses from all sin – including suicide. They are with Christ. Purified, holy and happy. Their minds and bodies tortured no more.

'For the Lamb at the centre of the throne will be their shepherd; 'he will lead them to springs of living water." 'And God will wipe away every tear from their eyes'" (Revelation 7:17).

CONSIDER: How would you help someone who confided in you that they had suicidal thoughts? What would you do if you felt like killing yourself? Who could you speak to?

RECOMMENDED FURTHER READING:
A Relentless Hope - Surviving the Storm of Teen Depression - Gary Nelson

PRAYER: Lord Jesus, there is no pit so deep, that you have not been there already. You cried out in the depths of despair, 'My God, my God, why have you forsaken me?' You understand. You know. Lord help us when we struggle with such dark despair. Help our friends and family. And may we always look to you to lift us out of the pit. Amen.

22. THOSE WHO HAVE NOT HEARD

QUESTION: What happens to babies who die before they have had the chance to become a Christian and people who have never heard of God?

BIBLE READING: Genesis 18:16-33

TEXT: Far be it from you to do such a thing—to kill the righteous with the wicked, treating the righteous and the wicked alike. Far be it from you! Will not the Judge of all the earth do right? (Genesis 18:25)

I love the story of Abraham pleading with the Lord for Sodom and Gomorrah. God has just told him that the sin of these two cities was so great that he was going to destroy them. Abraham is concerned that innocent people will be swept away. Fair enough says the Lord ... if there are fifty righteous people? ... But says Abraham, as he begins to haggle as though he were bargaining in a market, what if there are five less than fifty? ...

and so on until he gets down to ten. Abraham's plea was based upon one very important fact – 'Will not the judge of all the earth do right?'

That should be our starting and finishing point when we discuss this. God will do right. Right is what God does. The idea that we can sit in judgement upon God is a wicked one. He is the righteous one. We are not.

So what about babies who die before they have a chance to hear the gospel? Let's consider the story of David and Bathsheba in 2 Samuel 11 and 12. After David and Bathsheba had committed adultery, they had a child who became ill. David mourned, fasted and prayed for the child. But the child died. The servants were scared to tell him because they were worried how he would react. However, when he found out he got up, got washed and seemed to go back to normal life. 'Why are you acting this way?' they wondered.

'He answered, "While the child was still alive, I fasted and wept. I thought, 'Who knows? The Lord may be gracious to me and let the child live.' But now that he is dead, why should I go on fasting? Can I bring him back again? I will go to him, but he will not return to me"' (2 Samuel 12:22-23).

David was certain that he would go to his child.

Although the Bible tells us that all human babies are born in sin, yet it also says that the dead are judged according to what they have done (Revelation 20:12). My view is that this means that the blood of Jesus also covers the sins of those who die in infancy, before they have had the chance to do anything right or wrong. I once had to bury an eighteen-month-old child – who had died from a cot death. When you stand beside that tiny white coffin, with the weeping parents in front of you, there is no way that you think that this child has gone to hell, purgatory or limbo (as some churches teach). Surely the mercy and blood of Christ extends to these little ones?

But what about those who have not heard? Again we work on the principle that the judge of all the earth will do right. God is not going to judge people for not believing in a Christ of whom they have never heard! However, the Bible tells us that people are judged according to the light they have and what they have done with that light. Romans 1:18-23 makes it very clear that that light is sufficient for them to know God's eternal power and divine nature and yet they still continue to sin against that light. They need to hear about Jesus – not to save them from the sin of rejecting a Christ of whom they have never heard, but to save them from their sin against the God whom they do know, and whose law is written in their hearts. All people, throughout the entire world, need a Saviour. Which is why Jesus is the Saviour of the whole world.

Let's return to the basic foundation for answering and thinking about these kinds of questions. God is the judge of all the earth. He is righteous, good and just. As such he will do right. Our real question is not what God has done about others, but what we have done with the knowledge and understanding that we have of him. We must seek the Lord while he can be found.

CONSIDER: We know that God can do nothing wrong. The key question is what we do with what we know of God. Why do you think it is important to both examine yourself and to desire to tell others?

RECOMMENDED FURTHER READING:

This article from John Piper is a clear explanation to a twelve-year-old girl:

https://www.desiringgod.org/articles/what-about-those-who-have-never-heard

PRAYER: Lord God, you are the judge of all the earth and you will always do right. When we are tempted to doubt your goodness help us to remember that. Give us the boldness of Abraham in praying for others. Have mercy upon us. Have mercy upon your people. Have mercy upon our families and communities. O Lord, have mercy upon your world, in the name and for the sake of Jesus. Amen.

23. THE END OF THE WORLD

QUESTION: When is the world ending? What will happen after the world ends?

BIBLE READING: 2 Peter 3:1-18

TEXT: But the day of the Lord will come like a thief. The heavens will disappear with a roar; the elements will be destroyed by fire, and the earth and everything done in it will be laid bare (2 Peter 3:10).

Most people who read this won't be old enough to remember the beginning of the new millennium in the year 2000. There were lots of predictions of doom and disaster – even from secularists who were concerned and worried about the millennium bug. Every now and then a false prophet or cult leader will announce that the end of the world is due on April the 16th or whatever random date they choose. They will write books telling us how they have calculated this from the Bible (the thought always strikes me – why sell books and make money if the world is going to end?!). The Jehovah's Witnesses have for example predicted the end of the world, as we know it, several times – 1878, 1881, 1914, 1918, 1925 and 1975. I believe their latest prediction is now into the 2030s. With a track record like that I'm not sure why anyone continues to follow them!

The truth is that we don't know when the end of the world will happen. And Jesus didn't. *'But about that day or hour no one knows, not even the angels in heaven, nor the Son, but only the Father'* (Matthew 24:36). Some people think that can't be right because surely Jesus was God and God knows everything? But they forget that Jesus became human and limited himself not only to time and space, but also to our intellectual capacity. He had to learn. He wasn't walking around as a super know-it-all toddler! He says that the date of his return and the end of the world was not revealed to him, and therefore it was not revealed to his disciples. We don't know.

There does seem to be a great fascination with the end of the world. That's why we get all these apocalyptic end-of-the-world Sci-Fi movies. Are we going to be hit by a giant comet, zapped by aliens from outer space, wiped out by a super bug, or just blow ourselves up?! Again some Christians seem to fall into the trap of not only speculating about when the end of the world will occur, but they think they can tell us exactly what will happen. They use the apocalyptic literature of the Bible – Ezekiel, Daniel, Revelation and some other parts and often present us with a great scheme of things which usually focuses around their country and people they know of! Again, as with all things biblical, it is better for us neither to add nor take away from the Bible. Let's just take the simple and plain lessons we get from our chapter today – 2 Peter 3.

Jesus is returning. Even though people scoff and mock and ask when it will happen – there is no doubt that he will return. He is being patient wanting everyone to come to repentance (v. 9). If a day with the Lord is like a thousand years then we are only two days away from his first coming.

The day of the Lord will result in a great destruction but also a great renewal of the heavens and the earth. We are looking forward to a new heaven and a new earth. Evil will be removed from this renewed universe.

This hope makes us live for Christ on this earth – as we anticipate the new universe. We make every effort to be found 'spotless, blameless and at peace with him' (v. 14). The teaching about the second coming is not meant for speculative books or films, but rather to inspire us to holiness – to become more like Christ. We are to grow in the grace and knowledge of our Lord Jesus Christ. Such a hope makes us call out 'Maranatha' [Come soon, Lord Jesus], (1 Corinthians 16:22).

CONSIDER: Why is it dangerous and wrong to speculate about the end of the world? Do you live your life in anticipation of Christ's return? What difference should it make to your life knowing that he is coming back?

RECOMMENDED FURTHER READING:
How will the World End? – Jeramie Rinne

PRAYER: Maranatha – even so come soon Lord Jesus. We live in a world that was created so beautiful by you. We still see so much of that beauty – but we are also conscious of the great darkness that covers the earth. We long for the day when you will restore and renew the heavens and the earth. Meanwhile we wait for you – and we pray that you would make us ready for that day. Amen.

24. REINCARNATION

QUESTION: If we are eternal beings how can the spirit/soul have a start point? Are ideas of reincarnation and transmigration more plausible?

BIBLE READING: John 5:16-30

TEXT: Do not be amazed at this, for a time is coming when all who are in their graves will hear his voice and come out—those who have done what is good will rise to live, and those who have done what is evil will rise to be condemned (John 5:28-29).

The Buddhist teaching about reincarnation has been very influential throughout the world. Even in the traditionally Christian West it has had an impact. In one sense it seems to make sense and seems so fair. When this life is over our karma is to be reborn into another one – not necessarily a human one. Whether we have been good or bad will determine where we are reborn. Buddhists believe there are six realms, Gati, which

103

they call Bhavachakra – the heavenly, the demi-god, human, animals, ghosts and hell.

Transmigration is the view that the soul moves into another body. So if you think that your dog is your reincarnated granny then you believe in transmigration.

From a biblical perspective does this make any sense? In the Hindu religion the soul does not have a beginning nor an end. It is eternal, immortal and ageless. But the Bible teaches that every soul has a beginning – because only God is eternal. We come into being. He *is* being. God breathed into the man and the man became a living soul. As the psalmist says our inmost being was knit together when we were in our mother's womb.

'For you created my inmost being; you knit me together in my mother's womb' (Psalm 139:13).

The Bible is clear that we have a beginning. But are we immortal? Do we have no end? There are lots of reports in newspapers about how one day scientists are going to make us immortal and we need never die. That is a fantasy. From a Christian perspective we know that God alone has immortality (1 Timothy 6:16). But perhaps in the creation when God breathed into the soul of mankind and set eternity in our hearts, he made us immortal souls?

If you look at what Jesus said in our passage, he is telling us that we are going to be raised and we are going to face judgement. The writer to the Hebrews tells us the same thing: *'Just as people are destined to die once, and after that to face judgement'* (Hebrews 9:27).

The point is that we were not just made for this life, but we were made for an eternal existence. We are going to be raised from the dead and we are going to be judged by an Almighty God. We are not going to be reincarnated and our soul is not going to transmigrate elsewhere.

What should really concern us is what will happen to us on the day of judgement. Jesus tells us that those who have done good will rise to live, and those who have done evil will rise to be condemned. This is not a kind of Christian Karma – as so many seem to believe – where if you do good things on earth you get a nice reward in heaven, but if you do bad things you go to hell. What Jesus is referring to here is the good that he says God requires of human beings – to believe in the one he has sent (John 6:29). The evil is to reject God and to reject the one he has sent. It is on that one issue that all our judgement lies. Either we are clothed in the righteousness and goodness of Christ, or we choose to stand before God in our own righteousness, which the Bible describes as 'filthy rags'.

The Scottish band, *The Proclaimers*, are famous for their song '500 miles'. But they have a song which I like even better which addresses this issue – It's called 'The More I Believe'. Here are some of the relevant words:

I don't believe in beads or crystals
Instant karma or mother earth
I don't believe that what I think
Makes any difference to what I'm worth

I don't believe in reincarnation
I'm not coming back as a flower
I don't bow my head to kings or priests
'Cause I believe in your higher power
The less I believe in me

The more I believe in thee
The less I believe in me
The more I believe in thee.[16]

CONSIDER: Why is the doctrine of reincarnation such a hard doctrine? Can you see the difference between it and the Christian teaching of being saved through the grace of Christ?

RECOMMENDED FURTHER READING:

Jesus Among Other Gods (Youth Edition) – Ravi Zacharias

PRAYER: Lord God, we bless you that you have made us in your image and that you breathed your Spirit into us. We thank you that we are not caught in an endless cycle of Karma but that one day we will be raised and those who believe in you, will really live. We pray that each of us would love and trust you completely and not rely on our own good works, in the name of Jesus. Amen.

---

16. *The More I Believe*, Craig Reid and Charles Reid; Label: Parlophone Album: Hit the Highway, released 1994.

25. THE PURPOSE OF LIFE

QUESTION: Why did God create us? What is the meaning of life?

BIBLE READING: Ephesians 2:1-10

TEXT: For we are God's handiwork, created in Christ Jesus to do good works, which God prepared in advance for us to do (Ephesians 2:10).

This is one of those questions that many of us think that we can answer easily – or that we already know. We find our purpose in our day-to-day existence and yet sometimes when we think a bit deeper, we find ourselves asking what are we really here for? The psalmist, after looking at the power of God in creation, has a look at humanity and asks, 'What is humanity? Why do you care for them?' (Psalm 8).

Let's begin by getting rid of one wrong answer. God did not create us because he needed us, or because he was lonely. When Paul addressed the philosophers in Athens he told them:

'The God who made the world and everything in it is the Lord of heaven and earth and does not live in temples built by human hands. And he is not served by human hands, as if he needed anything. Rather, he himself gives everyone life and breath and everything else' (Acts 17:24-25).

He then goes on to tell us that God created us and appointed where we should live, so that we might seek him and reach out for him. In other words he created us for relationship with himself.

Augustine put it beautifully: 'Thou hast made us for thyself, O Lord, and our heart is restless until it finds its rest in thee.'[17] The Westminster Shorter Catechism has for its first question: 'What is man's chief end?' (i.e. what is our purpose? why were we made?). The answer? 'Man's chief end is to glorify God and enjoy him forever.' I love that answer. What a great purpose! When God made us he saw that we were 'very good'. We were the epitome of his creation. We were made in his image. Our purpose is thus to show who he is and reveal his glory – even more than the stars and the heavens. And we are to enjoy him. This is not to be a relationship of servitude and fear, but of love and son/daughtership! As John Piper states, 'God is most glorified in us when we are most satisfied in him.'

But as our passage in Ephesians tells us – we are no longer fit for purpose. Humanity has rebelled and now we are 'dead in sins and trespasses' as we glory in the ways of this sinful world, rather than in God. By nature, now, we are 'children of wrath',

---

17. Attributed to St Augustine of Hippo, A.D. 354-430.

deserving the punishment of God. And that is what we would remain if it were up to us. But God has not given up on us. He sent Jesus. When we become Christians we realise he made us alive with him. We are born again. We are saved – not because of anything we have done, but because of what he has done. This is a wonderful truth. And we are saved for a purpose. That we may be restored to our original purpose – glorifying God and enjoying him forever. We are 'created in Christ Jesus, to do good works, which God has prepared in advance for us to'.

This is so significant for our self-understanding and our lives. We don't have to earn our salvation; we don't have to prove ourselves. Not only can we not buy a stairway to heaven, we can't glorify God on our own. What he has done is given us new birth, given us a new life and he has even prepared in advance the good works that he wants us to do. Our task is simply to seek his will and to do it. He has given us his Word, his Spirit and his church, our brothers and sisters, to help us.

So the next time you wonder what your purpose is in life you can answer, 'It is to glorify God and enjoy him.' You can work out everything else from that. You know the story of the Scottish runner and missionary Eric Liddell – portrayed in the amazing film Chariots of Fire[18] (if you haven't seen it – get a copy!). When he was deciding to run for the Olympics his sister, Jenny, was concerned that he was forgetting God's call on him to be a missionary in China. He told her that he was still going to go to China and he was still supportive of the little mission work they had to do, but he was going to take a break and prepare for the race – why? 'I believe God made me for a purpose, but he also made me fast! And when I run I feel his pleasure.'

---

18. *Chariots of Fire*, 1981, Director: Hugh Hudson, 20th Century Fox.

When we do what God has called us to do; when we follow Jesus and live for his glory in all that we do – then whatever we do – we feel his pleasure.

CONSIDER: Are you aware of God's primary calling on your life – to seek him, to reach out for him and to give your life to him? Can you think of things that you are doing now, which do not glorify God? Can you think of things that do? How do you know what is glorifying to God?

RECOMMENDED FURTHER READING:
Desiring God – John Piper

PRAYER: O Lord, our hearts were made for you, and they are restless until they find their rest in you. Grant all of us that holy restlessness. Never let us be satisfied with anything less than you. And enable us to live all our days glorifying and enjoying you. Amen.

26. RICH AND FAMOUS

QUESTION: I also want to become rich and famous, like celebrities – what am I to do?

BIBLE READING: 1 Timothy 6:3-21

TEXT: Those who want to get rich fall into temptation and a trap and into many foolish and harmful desires that plunge people into ruin and destruction. For the love of money is a root of all kinds of evil. Some people eager for money, have wandered from the faith and pierced themselves with many griefs (1 Timothy 6:9-10).

An African pastor wrote to me a heartfelt plea when he heard I was writing this book:

'Africans are encountering the challenge of poverty and dreaming of going to the West. The youth in Africa and particularly Burundi are encountering unemployment and go to the West where they hope there are green pastures. The prosperity gospel is taking advantage of the ill situation they are in and promising heaven on earth, scholarships, visas to the U.S. etc. The proponents of prosperity gospel are from the West, yet they are depleting even the remaining wealth'.

It is a matter of great shame to the Western church that we have allowed, encouraged and created an atmosphere in which the prosperity gospel teachers such as Benny Hinn, Joyce Meyer, Creflo Dollar and numerous other tele-evangelists flourish. It is even worse that we have exported the prosperity gospel to African countries where some African pastors now exploit their own people. In a recent survey it was found that half of the top ten richest pastors in the world are in Nigeria. A Nigerian friend came to me and told me that he was really struggling with Christianity because his mother, who was poor, had recently saved $100 so that she could pay a local preacher to come and bless her house with holy water! Little wonder that he struggled.

Such false teachers need to read our passage today. The prosperity gospel is not from God. It is the very opposite of what Paul teaches Timothy. The prosperity gospel uses a very worldly logic that argues that God wants you to be rich rather than poor, he wants you to be healthy rather than sick, he wants you to prosper rather than struggle. So if you are poor, sick or struggling then it must be the devil, or your lack of faith. The prosperity gospel teacher then tells you that he/she can help you if you 'sow your seed' (give them money), and show you how godliness is a way to make money.

Paul tells us that such teachers have been robbed of the truth. They have fallen into foolish and harmful desires which plunge people into ruin and destruction. They have wandered from the faith and, despite appearances of blessing and prosperity; they have pierced themselves with many griefs.

The Bible does not say it is wrong to have wealth, but it does say that it is a temptation and a snare. It warns those who are rich in this world not to put their hope in wealth, but rather in God, who richly provides us with everything for our enjoyment. We are to lay up treasure in heaven and not on earth.

The early Christian church did not have many rich, noble and privileged people within it (although it did have some). The message of Jesus was way too radical for them. The church in the West has distorted and perverted that message – even many of us who do not accept the prosperity gospel are guilty of that. Unless we repent of our materialism, greed and sinful trust in riches the Church in the West will go the way that the Church in Turkey and the Church in North Africa went in the past. The future of the church appears to be in Africa, Asia and South America.

I hope and pray that our African brothers and sisters will lead us in the future into a better expression of the wonderful gospel of Jesus Christ. Please don't fall for the heresies that are a cancer on the body of Christ in the West.

None of this is to take away from the poverty and pain of the unemployed and poor in Burundi or other countries. But those who are Christians in these countries should not flee to the West seeking wealth, but rather stay and work as Jesus called us to, as salt and light in our own communities. Imagine an Africa with rulers, business leaders, academics and pastors who were not using Christianity as a means to gain wealth and power, but instead as a means to serve and empower others!

That would be the world turned upside down. That is your calling. Use whatever God has given you to glorify him in this world, to seek justice and to be a blessing to the poor.

CONSIDER: Why has the prosperity gospel been so popular in the West and also in Africa? What is wrong with it? What is the good news for the poor?

RECOMMENDED FURTHER READING:
Money Counts – Graham Benyon

PRAYER: O God, you are good and the giver of good. You richly give us all things to enjoy. We pray that if we have lots of material things we will not trust in them, we will not horde them, but instead use them for your glory. If we are poor, we ask, O Lord, that you would give us our daily bread and that we would learn to trust you for everything. Take away from us the desire to be rich, and help us to see that we are rich in you and through you can do all things! Help us to fight the good fight of the faith, in the name of the one who for our sakes became poor, that we might become truly rich. Amen.

27. BEING A CHRISTIAN

QUESTION: What is being a Christian anyway?

BIBLE READING: Acts 11:19-30

TEXT: Then Barnabas went to Tarsus to look for Saul, and when he found him, he brought him to Antioch. So for a whole year Barnabas and Saul met with the church and taught great numbers of people. The disciples were called Christians first at Antioch (Acts 11:25-26).

The name 'Christian' is used in different ways – so much so that sometimes it almost seems as though it is meaningless. Lots of people will call themselves Christians – even if they don't go to church, read or believe the Bible. They understand it to mean being a 'good person' (that's not very 'Christian' of you) or as belonging to a particular culture (I am a Christian rather than a Muslim, Buddhist, Hindu or Atheist). But that is not what the name means.

The term 'Christian' is used only three times in the Bible. First of all, in our passage where we read that the disciples were first called Christians at Antioch (in Syria). Note that this was not a name they gave to themselves. It was a nickname (probably mocking) given to them by others. 'See, these followers of Christ (the one who was crucified), these Christians.' Luke records this because by the time he came to write Acts, 'Christian' was becoming an increasingly used term. Before this they saw themselves as 'disciples' or 'saints' or 'brothers'. But the name Christian stuck – even though it was largely seen as an insult – in much the same way that when I was at school the Christians were called 'Bible-bashers' or 'the holy joes'.

The second time the term 'Christian' is used is when Paul was on trial before King Agrippa. In defending himself Paul went on the offensive and proclaimed the gospel and challenged King Agrippa.

'Then Agrippa said to Paul, "Do you think that in such a short time you can persuade me to be a Christian?"' (Acts 26:28).

Perhaps there is an edge of contempt and fear in this assertion as Agrippa was scared of being persuaded and did not want to become one of the dreaded Christians. Paul's answer was brilliant:

'Paul replied, "Short time or long—I pray to God that not only you but all who are listening to me today may become what I am, except for these chains"' (Acts 26:29).

The third and final time the name Christian is used is by Peter in his first letter.

'However, if you suffer as a Christian, do not be ashamed, but praise God that you bear that name.' (1 Peter 4:16).

Again it is clear that being perceived as a Christian was not praise but a term of contempt. Being a Christian involved suffering.

So what is being a Christian? A Christian is someone who follows Jesus Christ. Not just some of his teachings, but all of them. Nor do we just follow his teachings from the past – we follow him as a living Lord today. We don't follow a dead Jesus but a risen Saviour. We don't follow him as an equal but we acknowledge him as Lord. A Christian is someone who declares with their mouth, 'Jesus is Lord', and believes in their heart that God raised Jesus from the dead (Romans 10:9). A Christian is someone who is saved. And a Christian is someone who will suffer. Jesus warned us:

'... *If they persecuted me, they will persecute you also'* (John 15:20).

The world doesn't want real Christianity and real Christians. They want the adverb 'Christian' to mean 'nice'. They want the noun 'Christian' to mean 'a nice person who does nice things and goes along with what we say'. But a real Christian is a disciple of Jesus (following him); filled with the Holy Spirit (we are 'saints' – the holy ones – the ones called to be holy); united with other believers (we are brothers and sisters who belong to one body – the Church of Jesus Christ through all ages and all the world); and united to him (the favourite description of a Christian to Paul is someone who is 'in Christ'). So you can see it is much more than culture, much more than tradition, much more than religion. To be a Christian is to be ransomed, healed, restored, forgiven. To be a Christian is to be born again, to be a new creation, to receive a new life. To be a Christian is the greatest thing in the world.

And it is all of the mercy, goodness and love of God, that we can be called by the name of his Son.

CONSIDER: What is the difference between real Christianity and fake Christianity? How do you become a Christian? How would you know if you are a real Christian?

RECOMMENDED FURTHER READING:
Basic Christianity – John Stott

PRAYER Lord Jesus, you are the Christ, the promised Messiah. You came to die for your people and to purchase them for your glory as your Bride. It is the greatest thing in the world to be called by your name, even if the world uses it as mockery. Grant that I may truly be a Christian and worthy of your name. Cleanse me, forgive me, renew me and fill me with your Holy Spirit. Amen.

28. RELIGION AND BIRTH

QUESTION: Does your religion depend on where you were born?

BIBLE READING: John 1:1-18

TEXT: He came to that which was his own, but his own did not receive him. Yet to all who did receive him, to those who believed in his name, he gave the right to become children of God—children born not of natural descent, nor of human decision or a husband's will, but born of God (John 1:11-13).

What language do you speak? I suspect the language of your parents! I also suspect that you have many of the tastes, opinions and even mannerisms of your parents. Is that the same for religion? What is known as 'the geography argument' certainly at first glance seems to make sense. If you were born in Saudi Arabia you would be Muslim, if you were born in India you will be Hindu, if you were born in America you will be Christian. Therefore, religion is just a matter of culture and where you are born, not a matter of truth or God. So we might as well all be atheists!

Except ... surely the same argument applies to atheists? If you were born in an atheist country like China then you are more likely to be atheist or in a secularist country, like Sweden, you are more likely to be secular humanist. Does that invalidate atheism and secular humanism?

The argument also fails because there are people born in Saudi Arabia who do not end up as Muslims, likewise in India there are millions of Muslims and Christians as well as atheists and secular humanists. And I know many Swedish Christians.

It also fails because it presupposes that culture and family are the sole determining factors. It does not allow for people changing their minds, being converted or for the possibility of supernatural conversion. In other words the argument is based upon presuppositions which themselves are not self-evident. It is a circular self-defeating argument.

However, it is clear that religion does depend to a large extent on your culture, your environment, your family and where you are born. But your relationship with God does not. That is the key difference.

That is what John chapter one teaches us. Jesus, the light of the world, came as the light to the whole world. He came to his own people (the Jews), but they rejected him. Yet to all who will receive him, who believe in his name, he gives the right to become children of God – children born not of natural descent, nor of human decision or a husband's will, but born of God. This means that being a Christian, becoming a child of

God, is not primarily dependent on our environment, or place of birth. It is dependent upon hearing about, and responding to, the gospel of Jesus Christ.

There are countries and communities where we are more likely to hear and experience the gospel. Those who are brought up in such a privileged environment should be thankful and should not abuse their privilege. How can they hear without a preacher? But the great thing about the gospel is that it has gone into all the world and it is producing fruit all over the world. The notion that Christianity is primarily a white European religion is a false one. The vast majority of Christians are now in Africa, China and South America.

Sometimes being brought up in a nominally Christian society can actually do more harm than good to our spiritual health. What we experience as Christianity is not the real thing at all. It's a little like getting the flu jag, which gives you enough of the flu to immunize you from getting the real thing.

And let's not forget the Holy Spirit. No one – whatever their upbringing – can even see the kingdom of God unless they are born from above, of the Spirit (John 3). Many people have been brought from death to life who were not born or brought up in a Christian context. I think of a Muslim friend who was brought to faith in Jesus through a dream, a Chinese communist who came to believe through visiting a church, and a Hindu who heard about Jesus from a cult and started to read the Bible for himself. The gospel will be preached to all the nations and the Spirit of Jesus will not be constrained by our cultures.

CONSIDER: Given that background is such an important part of our lives, why is it not the determining factor for our faith?

RECOMMENDED FURTHER READING:
The Reason for God – Tim Keller

PRAYER: Lord Jesus, you came as the light of the world, to all the people of the world. Help us to receive you, to believe in you, whatever our upbringing. If we have Christian parents and have grown up in the Christian church, we bless you for that privilege, but we know that that will not save us. So we come to you. If we have heard of you from others, we bless you for those you have sent to tell us and to invite us to become your children. May your gospel and Word flourish and prosper throughout the whole of your world – to the glory of your name. Amen.

29. HITLER

BIBLE READING: Ezekiel 18

TEXT: The one who sins is the one who will die. The child will not share the guilt of the parent, nor will the parent share the guilt of the child. The righteousness of the righteous will be credited to them, and the wickedness of the wicked will be charged against them (Ezekiel 18:20).

It is astonishing how many times Hitler comes up in conversation. It's not just that people have a seemingly endless fascination with him; it's the way that the new fundamentalist atheists have adopted 'Hitler was a Christian' as one of their mantras. So how do we answer this one?

Certainly not just by saying, 'No he wasn't, he was an atheist.' Nor is it helpful to shrug one's shoulders and walk away from the discussion, as though it did not matter. Because if Hitler was inspired by Christianity to do what he did, there is a serious charge to answer.

If you are asking whether Hitler was a follower of Jesus Christ, the answer is absolutely no. If you mean, was he baptised as a Catholic and did he sometimes make positive references to Christianity in his public speeches, and did he try to get the churches on his side, then yes. But he was not a Christian in any meaningful sense of the word. He did not read the Bible, go to church, or follow Jesus. He hated God's chosen people, the Jews. It is difficult to see how someone who hated the Jews could follow the greatest Jew of all. As his ideologue Martin Bormann put it: 'National Socialism (Nazism) and Christianity are irreconcilable ... National Socialism is based on scientific foundations ... [It] must always, if it is to fulfil its job in the future, be organised according to the latest knowledge of scientific research.' He condemns 'the concepts of Christianity, which in their essential points have been taken over from Jewry'.[19]

But the fact that Hitler was not a Christian does not answer our question: Why did God make Hitler? The question itself is a bit strange – because God does not make people out of a mould, and programme them to do all the good or evil they do. In addition, we should be enormously thankful that Hitler and the Nazis were ultimately defeated. Is it not a bit inconsistent for people to blame God for Hitler but not to thank him for Hitler's defeat?

If the questioner is suggesting that God should not permit anyone to be born who would do evil – then would that not eradicate most, if not all of us? We are really back

---

19. From an article, *Was Hitler really a Christian?*, Christian Today, 10 June 2016.

to the age-old question of suffering – except this time on a massive scale.

The most we can say is that God let the German people and the European nations go their own way. They decided to reject God and Christianity and become a 'modern', 'advanced' nation. As a result they ended up with Hitler. And remember that Hitler was just one individual, a figurehead for an evil that was to do with far more than he. The question I asked when I was a teenager (and I read loads of books about Hitler, Weimar Germany and the Nazis – I even went to the University of Edinburgh to study that subject), was how could this happen? How could the most advanced, sophisticated and cultured nation in the world end up being led by someone like Hitler? The answer for me was frightening – there is a heart of darkness within every human being – including me. And yet out of the evil came hope.

The concentration camp in Auschwitz was, for me, one of the reasons I became a Christian. It proves the Bible's teaching that if human beings are left to their own devices they will make a mess and a hell of things. As Freddie Mercury, late of Queen, sang at the first Live Aid, 'If there's a God up above, a God of love, then what must he think, of the mess that we've made, of the world that he created?'[20]

A couple of years ago I stood at the gates of Auschwitz in tears. It was not just the industrial scale of man's inhumanity to man, but also the answer to how to deal with that, which overwhelmed me. Ultimately, the atheist world view has no

---

20. *Is this the world we created*, Freddie Mercury and Brian May.
Greenpeace – the album released June 1985. Issued on Greenpeace records, Distributed by EMI/Parlophone Capitol, Hollywood Reocords.

answer to the problem of evil, as exemplified in the Holocaust. But Christianity does. And that answer is Christ. His life, love, teaching, death and atonement. If Hitler and the German people had followed Christ, there would have been no holocaust. The fact that they did not do so is not God's fault. As our text says – we are responsible for our own sin.

CONSIDER: Why do you think Hitler and the Nazis were able to gain power? Why was there such a hatred of the Jews? What do you think will happen to humanity if God just leaves us to get on with things?

RECOMMENDED FURTHER READING:
Hitler's Religion – The Twisted Beliefs that Drove the Third Reich – Richard Weikart

PRAYER: Lord God, how the nations rage? How they mock and scorn and oppress your people. We cry, how long O Lord, how long? We long to be delivered from evil. Deliver us from the evil within and the evil without. Keep us from the evil one and break the strength of wicked men, in Jesus' name. Amen.

30. RACISM

QUESTION: Why did God make the whites superior to us Africans and they even made us their slaves and colonized us and even now they look at us like we are apes or not humans or slaves or stupid (not intelligent like them)?

BIBLE READING: Acts 17:16-34

TEXT: From one man he made all the nations, that they should inhabit the whole earth; and he marked out their appointed times in history and the boundaries of their lands. God did this so that they would seek him and perhaps reach out for him and find him, though he is not far from any one of us. 'For in him we live and move and have our being.' As some of your own poets have said, 'We are his offspring' (Acts 16:26-28).

The problem here is not with God but with man. God did *not* make the whites superior to Africans. He made all human beings equally in his image. The trouble is that we have turned away from God and as a result have turned on one another.

'What causes fights and quarrels among you? Don't they come from your desires that battle within you?' (James 4:1).

The question is more, why were the European nations able to conquer most of the world? And why did they enslave some people? Again none of this is new – as the Bible indicates – slavery has always been a part of fallen human culture. Over a million white Europeans were enslaved by Arab traders in the Middle Ages. Africans enslaved and sold one another. In the seventeenth and eighteenth centuries, European slave traders took millions of Africans to the West Indies and America to staff their plantations. It was a shameful and disgusting trade that only ended after the campaigns led by that great Christian reformer, William Wilberforce. Missionaries like David Livingstone and Mary Slessor from my own country were instrumental in campaigning against slavery within Africa.

But slavery still exists in different forms today. There are people who are trafficked as sex slaves – tens of thousands of people throughout the world are enslaved in this way. There are other milder forms. When rich countries like my own can't get people to do what we consider demeaning or hard jobs, we import people from poorer countries, pay them less and exploit them. That is a kind of 'wage slavery'.

But what you are also asking is why some white people consider themselves to be superior to other races – especially Africans. Racism exists in every culture. Racism is the belief that just because of our skin colour we are superior. White racism today is not so much tied in with skin colour but with a kind of social Darwinian view that the highest evolution of the human species are largely white middle-class liberals.

Social Darwinism stemmed from Darwin's theory of evolution. Did you know that the full title of his influential work *The Origin of the Species* was *On the Origin of Species by Means of Natural Selection, or the Preservation of Favoured Races in the Struggle for Life?* Those who accepted Darwinian evolution naturally thought that their race (white European) was the favoured race. This has had incredibly harmful consequences. I am writing this from Australia where, at the beginning of the twentieth century, white Europeans hunted aboriginal people as though they were animals.

One of the most extreme examples of this I have come across is the nineteenth-century writer H.G. Wells; famous for books like *The Invisible Man* and *War of the Worlds*. In his *New Republic* he answered the question as to how the New Republic would deal with the 'inferior races' such as the black, the yellow man etc. He stated, 'Well, the world is a world, and not a charitable institution, and I take it they will have to go.'[21] He made it quite clear what he meant – the extermination of inferior races. Here was a white liberal progressive arguing that because other races were inferior they would have to go.

Of course today all liberal progressives would shout out loud their anti-racist credentials and how they believe that all humans are equal. But I'm not sure on what rational basis they base this. It is only Christianity with its view that all human beings are created in the image of God that provides a real basis for equality and diversity.

I think that you will still find that most white liberal progressives believe that their culture is superior and should

---

21. *Anticipations of the Reaction of Mechanical and Scientific Progress Upon Human Life and Thought*, H.G. Wells, The North American Review Publishing Co., 1901.

be imposed upon the rest of the world. That is why you often get Western 'charities' or government agencies giving aid to Africa with conditions attached. They want to impose their views on issues such as abortion and sexuality on all the countries of the world. I once received a letter from the Ghanaian ambassador to the United Kingdom thanking me for speaking up for his country and pointing out as you did, that so many in the West seem to think that the West is superior and African countries backward. My view is that the Western countries are sinking backwards into a Greco/Roman/Pagan view of the world. My hope and prayer is that the African countries will not follow us but rather lead us back to Christianity. We need more missionaries from Africa. Come over and help us.

CONSIDER: How can we combat the challenge and sin of racism? How can African nations grow and develop as Western nations decline?

RECOMMENDED FURTHER READING:
Mary Slessor – A Life on the Altar for God – Bruce McLennan

PRAYER: Our Father in heaven, we thank you that all human beings are made in your image. We thank you that you have created us in different races and placed us in different nations – that all might reach out for you and find you. Lord, forgive us when we are racist and think that because of our skin colour or culture we are superior to others. Bless the people of Africa and continue to bring many in that wonderful continent to know, love and serve you, in Jesus' name. Amen.

31. NORTH KOREA

QUESTION: How would Jesus respond to North Korea?

BIBLE READING: Isaiah 40:1-20

TEXT: Surely the nations are like a drop in a bucket;
they are regarded as dust on the scales;
he weighs the islands as though they were fine dust
(Isaiah 40:15).

This question was asked by someone from South Korea, who understandably is concerned about the tensions and the potential threat from a dictatorial regime to the North, armed with nuclear weapons.

The question is always difficult because when we ask WWJD (What Would Jesus Do) we are really asking what should we do? – because we want to be like Jesus. In general though, I think that is an unwise way to think. God has given us his standards and laws in his Word and it is better for us to apply them to our own circumstances – rather than speculate on the basis of what Jesus would do, because a) we don't know and b) Jesus is different from us. We should be asking what does Jesus want us to do.

In terms then of what we should do, I would suggest the following:

We pray - *'I urge, then, first of all, that petitions, prayers, intercession and thanksgiving be made for all people— for kings and all those in authority, that we may live peaceful and quiet lives in all godliness and holiness'* (1 Timothy 2:1-2).

So we should pray for the leaders of North and South Korea, the U.S., China and Russia. We pray that we may be able to live peaceful and quiet lives in all godliness and holiness.

We love our enemies - That is what Jesus taught us to do. We should be seeking their salvation, not their destruction.

We communicate the gospel - John Ross was a missionary from my own area, the Scottish East Highlands. He was the first person to translate the Bible into Korean. The people of North Korea experienced a great revival in 1907. We long for them to experience that again. Who will go today?

I am sure that is what Jesus would want us to do. But what would he do? Remember that he is King of kings and Lord of lords, before whom, one day every knee will bow. As we see in our text - the nations are just a drop in the bucket to him. Sometimes the Lord's people forget who the Lord is and become overwhelmed by the power and strength of those who are arrayed against us. We see how small and weak we are, and how great and powerful the mighty nations appear to be. Yet they are just a drop in the bucket to the Lord. Whatever the appearance before our eyes in this world - we need to remember the reality.

Also remember that our God is so sovereign, wise and powerful that he can even use dictators and evil rulers for his own glory. King Cyrus, for example, in the seventh century B.C., was used to deliver and help the Jewish people. I remember well when President Ceausescu of Romania, not only oppressed and robbed his own people, but also sought to destroy churches. Within a year he had been overthrown and executed (1989). Things in this world can change very quickly. So quickly, that by the time this is printed the situation in Korea may already have changed.

We know that Jesus will return and that all the kings, leaders and people of this earth will bow down to him. That includes the leaders of North Korea, who seem to think that they are gods. One day they will find that there is only one King of kings. Meanwhile we pray, trust and work to spread the Good News of Jesus Christ – not only because that extends his Kingdom and results in the salvation of millions, but because it is also the most revolutionary movement in history. The world is turned upside down, as the gospel is proclaimed and people are changed. That is what Jesus will do for North Korea.

CONSIDER: Are you ever scared, confused, depressed and discouraged by what is going on in the world? How does faith in Jesus Christ help you? What is the importance of understanding and believing in the sovereignty and power of God? What is the best thing you can do for North Korea and other countries that are ruled by dictators?

RECOMMENDED FURTHER READING:

The Korean Pentecost – Bruce Hunt and William Blair

PRAYER: Sovereign Lord, the nations are as nothing to you. They are just a drop in the bucket. Even when the rulers of this world gather together and mock you, you laugh. We pray that you would break the arm of the wicked man. We pray that you would protect your people. O Lord, you are the Prince of Peace, grant us peace in our time and grant peace and prosperity in Korea. We pray for our brothers and sisters there, in Jesus' name. Amen.

32. DIVISION AND PEACE

QUESTION: Why should I follow Christianity when it has caused so much division in my own country?

BIBLE READING: Ephesians 2:11-22

TEXT: For he himself is our peace, who has made the two groups one and has destroyed the barrier, the dividing wall of hostility, by setting aside in his flesh the law with its commands and regulations. His purpose was to create in himself one new humanity out of the two, thus making peace, and in one body to reconcile both of them to God through the cross, by which he put to death their hostility. He came and preached peace to you who were far away and peace to those who were near (Ephesians 2:14-17).

This question comes from Northern Ireland which, for anyone who knows a little of the history of that troubled land, makes it a very understandable question. The 'Troubles' in Northern Ireland were often presented as a clash between two versions of Christianity – Roman Catholicism and Protestantism. But it is never just as simple as that. Politics, economics, history, family and tradition were all just as much factors. Sometimes religion was only used as a cover. For example the IRA were supposed to be the 'Catholic' terrorists, yet they were a Marxist group which de facto does not believe in God. There is an old joke about a man in Belfast being asked, 'Do you believe in God?' 'No, I'm an atheist.' 'But what kind of atheist are you – a Protestant or Catholic atheist?'

However, it is too simple to say that the trouble in Northern Ireland, or in other troubled parts of the world which involve the church, has nothing to do with Christianity. The Bible teaches that though we are Christians we are still sinners and we are easily affected/infected by the culture we are in. We can also infect the culture. In Northern Ireland there have been biblical Christians who confused their Christianity with their culture and traditions and thus caused great harm to the gospel cause. All of us can do that. We need to make sure that we do not confuse the gospel with the historical, cultural and social impacts upon our society. The gospel does not change – the culture and context do.

There have always been divisions within society and there always will be. In the first century Paul was acutely aware of the division between Jews and Gentiles. He was a Jew who ended up being the apostle to the Gentiles. He had experienced the 'barrier, the dividing wall of hostility' and now knew the reconciliation and peace that comes through Jesus Christ. We must never forget that Jesus comes to bring peace. He is the prince of peace and the preacher of peace. As his followers we have to be the same.

There is a wrong use of Christianity that brings trouble and strife. That does not mean that we should reject Christianity. Just as the wrong use of money, family, politics, sport and sex do not mean that we should reject these good gifts from God! But there is a real sense in which real Christianity does cause or expose division. Jesus said:

'Do you think I came to bring peace on earth? No, I tell you, but division' (Luke 12:51).

Here he is not referring to the kind of tribalism and strife that leads to war or fighting between peoples, but rather to the division caused by the reactions to him. His message is a radical one that demands total commitment to him in a family that may well cause division. Imagine if you are brought up in a Muslim family and come to follow Jesus Christ – your family could disown you. But it's not just in a Muslim family. I have seen secular parents who were so angry that their children became believers, that they disowned them. I have seen children seek to get their father put in a mental hospital when he became a Christian! Christ causes division between those who accept him and those who will not. But that is him really exposing the fact that human beings are enemies to God and if they have hated Jesus, they will also hate his followers.

Those of us who are his followers are not to hate our enemies – indeed the opposite. One of Jesus' hardest commands is to love our enemies. Our battle is not against flesh and blood but against the principalities and powers of this dark world. So we pray for our enemies, proclaim the gospel to them and love them. God will judge – not us.

In this sense, real Christianity is the only force in the world that has ever brought real peace. If you want peace in your own life and want to work for peace in this world, you need to be become a follower of the Prince of Peace.

CONSIDER: What causes strife and trouble in the world? How is it possible to bring real peace and unity in a community? Can you think of little ways that you can help bring reconciliation? What role does the gospel play in this?

RECOMMENDED FURTHER READING:

Love your Enemies – John Piper

PRAYER: Lord Jesus, you are the Prince of Peace. We ask that you would give peace in our lives, families and communities. Where there is trouble, strife and hatred, help us to respond with love. Forgive us when we have been the cause of fights and enable us to know the blessedness of peacemakers, in your name. Amen.

33. SEX AND SAME SEX MARRIAGE

QUESTION: Is sex really bad? If yes how come some of the younger people I know do it and nothing ever happens to them? Is sex before marriage a sin? What does God say about SSM (Same Sex Marriage)?

BIBLE READING: 1 Thessalonians 4:1-8

TEXT: It is God's will that you should be sanctified: that you should avoid sexual immorality; that each of you should learn to control your own body in a way that is holy and honourable, not in passionate lust like the pagans, who do not know God; and that in this matter no one should wrong or take advantage of a brother or sister. The Lord will punish all those who commit such sins as we told you and warned you before. For God did not call us to be impure, but to live a holy life (1 Thessalonians 4:3-7).

The importance of this question to our culture is seen that this was the only question in this book that was asked from every continent. Sex, marriage and gender identity are so important to us because they are a big part of what makes us human beings. The question is also asked because the biblical teaching about this is under attack from many in the culture – and because this is an area where there is sometimes a great deal of hypocrisy in the church – with people saying one thing and doing another.

The Bible, however, is not confused in its teaching. So in one way the answer to your question is straightforward. Sex is not bad, because it is something that God has given to us. He made us male and female, and he made us with the ability to love, to express that love physically and to produce children through that act of love. The Bible does not regard sex as bad, or as dirty. Indeed the very opposite. It is sacred and holy.

However, although God is the giver of pleasure, the devil is the perverter of pleasure. Just because it feels good does not make it good. God has set the limits for sex. It should be within the context of marriage. Genesis tells us that sex unites a husband and wife in an intimate knowledge of one another. It is not a shameful thing.

'That is why a man leaves his father and mother and is united to his wife, and they become one flesh. Adam and his wife were both naked, and they felt no shame' (Genesis 2:24-25).

But instead of uniting a man and a woman as one flesh, when sex is used wrongly, it is perverted and ends up bringing disunity, harm, hatred and destruction. Paul tells the Galatian church:

'The acts of the flesh are obvious: sexual immorality, impurity and debauchery; idolatry and witchcraft; hatred, discord, jealousy, fits of

rage, selfish ambition, dissensions, factions and envy; drunkenness, orgies, and the like. I warn you, as I did before, that those who live like this will not inherit the kingdom of God (Galatians 5:19-21).

The appearance that people commit sexual sin and 'nothing ever happens to them' has nothing to say about whether it is right or wrong. Although I note in passing that when we do not use our bodies in the way that God intends, lots of things do happen; sexually transmitted diseases, broken relationships, destroyed families, perverted minds, pornography, rape, prostitution and tormented individuals. It is surely best for us to follow the Maker's instructions. It's also good to remember that no one gets away with anything, for one day we will have to answer to God, for all we have done.

But what about SSM? Does the Bible forbid two people of the same sex marrying each other? Yes. Jesus' teaching is very clear:

"'Haven't you read," he replied, *"that at the beginning the Creator 'made them male and female,' and said, 'For this reason a man will leave his father and mother and be united to his wife, and the two will become one flesh'* (Matthew 19:4-5).

Two men don't become one flesh. Two women don't become one flesh. And same sex marriages cannot fulfil one of the great purposes of marriage – the pro-creation of children. We don't have time to go into this, but there are enormous consequences for individuals and societies who go against our Father's instructions. He gives us these because he loves us – not because he hates us.

This does not mean that homosexuality is the worst sin, or that homosexual sinners are worse than heterosexual ones. Most sexual sins described in the Bible are not to do with homosexuality. But it does mean that all of us as Christians are to live sexually pure lives because we want to honour God with our bodies.

'Marriage should be honoured by all, and the marriage bed kept pure, for God will judge the adulterer and all the sexually immoral' (Hebrews 13:4).

'Flee from sexual immorality. All other sins a person commits are outside the body, but whoever sins sexually, sins against their own body. Do you not know that your bodies are temples of the Holy Spirit, who is in you, whom you have received from God? You are not your own; you were bought at a price. Therefore honour God with your bodies' (1 Corinthians 6:18-20).

CONSIDER: Why is this such a big issue in our culture? What is wrong with SSM? How can we live sexually pure lives? Why does it matter?

RECOMMENDED FURTHER READING:
Is God Anti-Gay? – Sam Alberry
Married for God – Christopher Ash

PRAYER: Lord Jesus, so many of us find this so hard, because we know that our lusts and desires overwhelm us. We bless you that you are faithful and just and if we confess our sins, you forgive us. Help us to understand what your Word says and to be doers as well as hearers. Grant us holiness and love, so that we would not desire sin and hatred, in your name. Amen.

34. PORNOGRAPHY

QUESTION: What does God say about porn? How can I break the habit of watching pornography or masturbating?

BIBLE READING: Matthew 5:27-30

TEXT: But I tell you that anyone who looks at a woman lustfully has already committed adultery with her in his heart (Matthew 5:28).

Sometimes people think that the teaching of Jesus is a lot softer than the teaching of 'the God of the Old Testament'. We have seen already that we are not to think about God like that, because it is completely false. The God of the Old Testament is the God and Father of our Lord Jesus Christ – and there is no difference – except in expression and revelation. Here is one instance where that is true. The teaching of Jesus about sex and adultery is far harder than that of the Old Testament. Whereas the seventh commandment simply says 'do not commit adultery', Jesus defines that not just as the physical act but also the roving eye and lustful heart. By that standard most, if not all people have broken this commandment.

This is also becoming an even bigger problem today because of the Internet. Whilst there are many good things the Internet has brought us, there are also a whole range of evil and demonic – none more so than pornography. When the printing press was invented, it was not long before it was being used both to publish Bibles and to print pornography. Until recent decades, that still meant that pornography had to be physically purchased and kept. But with the arrival of the Internet, pornography has become cheaply available at the push of a button. At one point it was reckoned that one third of all traffic on the Internet was associated with pornography. In my own city it was reckoned that some 40 per cent of 12-13 year old boys had watched extreme pornography on their mobiles. What do you think that does to their brains, bodies and future relationships?

Surely this does not affect Christians? Sadly this is not true. This is one of the major areas that causes many Christians to stumble and fall. Even pastors. The trouble is that at home, as we are working on our computers, all kinds of temptations are offered up to us. Sometimes it can be something we see inadvertently, then we become curious. Then it gets a real hold. A desire is planted within and when we give into that, rather than satisfying the desire, it only adds fuel to the fire.

How can I break my addiction to Internet porn? You state correctly that it is a habit. So how do we break such habits? Often the normal advice is to take a series of practical measures, but can I suggest that you begin with the knowledge of God? 'You, O God see me' (Genesis 16:13). There is nowhere you can go from his presence (Psalm 139). Remember then that you are watching porn in the presence of a holy God. That should certainly act as a disincentive! Would you watch porn if your mother was standing beside you? As regards some of the practical measures, can I suggest doing what Job did: *'I made a covenant with my eyes'* (Job 31:1)? Take this seriously. Get an accountability partner. Talk to your pastor. Put a block on your phone or computer. Don't indulge even soft-core porn. And fill your life with other things – above all the love and service of God. Get the expulsive power of a new affection!

What about masturbation? This also becomes a habit. Some Christians argue that it's not really a sin providing that it's not done with lustful thoughts – which I would think is somewhat impossible. It is anyway kind of sad, what John White calls 'Sex on a desert island'.[22] This is not the purpose for which God gave us our sexual desires. It's a bit like drinking salt water to get rid of your thirst. It only increases it. Having said that, this is not the kind of sin that should leave you crippled by guilt. There are many other sins in your life that are more important.

CONSIDER: What would you think of someone using your sister, friend, mother as an object for their sexual gratification? Why then would you use someone else's sister, friend and mother for your own? Do you have someone who can hold you accountable for what you watch on your phone or computer?

---

22. John White, *Eros Defiled: The Christian & Sexual Sin*, InterVarsity Press, 1977.

RECOMMENDED FURTHER READING:
Finally Free: Fighting for Purity With The Power of Grace – Heath Lambert
Closing the Window: Steps to Living Porn-Free – Tim Chester

PRAYER: O Lord, you are pure and holy. You are always with us. We can never hide from you. Help us to remember that and to have a godly fear. Help us to value and respect not only other people's bodies, but our own. Cleanse us and purify us. Fill our hearts with a holy love for you. Amen.

35. ISLAM AND LOVE

QUESTION: How can we address the issue of love in Christianity when we compare it with the love claimed by the Muslims, as they seem to be helping their followers more than Christianity does?

BIBLE READING: Matthew 5:38-48

TEXT: You have heard that it was said, 'Love your neighbour and hate your enemy.' But I tell you, love your enemies and pray for those who persecute you, that you may be children of your Father in heaven. He causes his sun to rise on the evil and the good, and sends rain on the righteous and the unrighteous. If you love those who love you, what reward will you get? Are not even the tax collectors doing that? And if you greet only your own people, what are you doing more than others? Do not even pagans do that? Be perfect, therefore, as your heavenly Father is perfect (Matthew 5:43-48).

Let's not begin with comparisons and perceptions of what we think is happening, but let's instead begin with what Christians are supposed to do. All people will know that we are the disciples of Christ if we have love for one another (John 13:35). If we see a brother or sister in need and have the means to help and don't do so, then the love of God is not in us (1 John 3:17). It's very clear.

But more than that, Christians are to reflect their Father in heaven who makes his sun shine on the just and unjust – we are to do the same. We don't just care for Christians, we are to seek to care for as many of the needy as we can.

In the early church there is a fascinating letter from someone called Julian the Apostate. He writes as a hostile witness about the Christians: 'Why then do we think that this is sufficient and do not observe how the kindness of Christians to strangers, their care for the burial of their dead, and the sobriety of their lifestyle has done the most to advance their cause? ... For it is disgraceful when no Jew is a beggar and the impious Galileans [the name given by Julian to Christians] support our poor in addition to their own.'[23]

But let's turn to what you are asking. You have observed that Muslims seem to look after their own better than Christians. I'm sure that is true in some cases, but I would be careful about making or accepting such a generalisation. We are to look after our own, but the Christian is held to a higher standard. Not only are we to try and care for others, but we are also to love our enemies and pray for those who persecute us (Matthew 5:44). The Quran says:

---

23. Letter to Arsacius by Julian the Apostate.

'And good and evil deeds are not alike. Repel evil with good. And he who is your enemy will become your dearest friend' (41:33-34).

That seems fine, but the problem is that there are over a hundred verses in the Quran which encourage Muslims to fight their enemy.

'And kill them wherever you find them, and turn them out from where they have turned you out. And Al-Fitnah [disbelief or unrest] is worse than killing ... but if they desist, then lo! Allah is forgiving and merciful. And fight them until there is no more Fitnah [disbelief and worshipping of others along with Allah] and worship is for Allah alone' (Quran 2:191-193).

It is a very different standard.

The Christian command is, as the late Christopher Hitchens pointed out, a ridiculous and impossible command. Indeed it could even be dangerous. But that is what we are to do. We believe that God, and God alone, will be the judge on the final day. Meanwhile, we are to turn the other cheek and to seek the good of those who attack us. That doesn't mean that we can't defend ourselves or those we love, but it does mean we don't seek revenge and we don't hate anyone. This is the real radical love that turns the world upside down. This is the perfection of the Father.

One final thought – when you complain about the lack of love in the church, you may well be right. But as a Christian you have the opportunity to do something about that. You can show and grow in love and provide some of what is missing. We can all grow in love.

CONSIDER: Do you think it is true that Muslims show more love to Muslims than Christians do to Christians? Why do you think that is? What is the higher standard that Christians are to seek to live up to? What do you think can help us to live to that standard?

RECOMMENDED FURTHER READING:

Revolution of Love and Balance – George Verwer
Seeking Allah, Finding Jesus – Nabeel Qureshi

PRAYER: O God, who is love, we acknowledge how far short we fall in the standards you call us to. Help us to love our brothers and sisters in Christ, help us to love the people in your world and help us to love those who are our enemies. Fill us with your love, that we may share and show that in the church and in the world, in your name. Amen.

36. TRANSGENDER

QUESTION: In a society that is becoming increasingly accepting of a transgender-related way of life how should we as Christians face the issue ... and can we have some biblical evidence?

BIBLE READING: Genesis 1:24-31

TEXT: So God created mankind in his own image,
in the image of God he created them;
male and female he created them (Genesis 1:27).

This is a massive issue in today's culture and for the church. At first glance that does not appear to be obvious because Gender Identity Disorder (GID) affects only 0.1 per cent of the population and therefore seems a rather minor matter. The problem is that under the Trojan horse of 'equality' or preventing bullying a whole philosophy and worldview is being smuggled in. This philosophy is anti-God and anti-human. It is known as Queer theory and argues that gender has nothing to do with biology and is just a social construct. In a very short space of time we have moved from this being about 'trans' gender (people feeling that they are a different gender to the body they are born in) to being about 'multi' gender and people being able to pick any one of numerous genders.

What is the Christian perspective on all this? Let's begin with our text. Humanity was created male and female, both in the image of God. There are no other genders. Human beings were the apex of God's creation – whereas most of the creation was seen as good – humanity was seen as very good. This is why the devil's number one aim is to destroy the creation by destroying humanity. He is seeking to undo the creation. That is why this ideology of multi-gender and gender fluidity is from the pit of hell. It is as much a sin as the sin of racism or misogyny.

This is NOT to say that transgender people are from the pit of hell. Indeed they are often the ones who suffer most because they have been fed this false teaching, which they have come to believe. The rates of suicide and self-harm amongst transgender people are about nineteen times that of others.

As Christians we are to treat all people, including those who suffer from GID, with respect, love and compassion because they are made in the image of God. We also recognize that in a fallen world there will be confused sexual and gender identities. Jesus for example recognized that there were those who are born eunuchs (Matthew 19:12).

Genesis 2:18-22 teaches along with our text that this gender distinction is not an incidental detail but a fundamental part of being human. It does matter that we are created male and female. We were meant to complement and help one another.

Removing that distinction, or blurring it with a hundred others, can only do great harm to individual humans and to society in general.

Christianity also teaches that our bodies matter:

'Do you not know that your bodies are temples of the Holy Spirit, who is in you, whom you have received from God? You are not your own; you were bought at a price. Therefore honour God with your bodies' (1 Corinthians 6:19-20).

We do not honour God with our bodies when we mutilate them, seek to change them or deny them.

As Christians we are also concerned with truth. Transgender ideology is an absolute lie and as such it is profoundly destructive. As Ryan T. Anderson states:

'The best biology, psychology, and philosophy all support an understanding of sex as a bodily reality, and of gender as a social manifestation of bodily sex. Biology isn't bigotry. Every human society has been organized around a recognition that men and women are different, and modern science shows that the differences begin with our DNA and development in the womb.'[24]

The ideology that teaches there are many genders and that we can choose them is not just odd and a curiosity – it is harmful. As it is taught and enforced in our schools, media, political and legal systems it will cause untold harm to children, women, sports, feminism, the poor and indeed the whole of society. It is our Christian responsibility to love those who suffer from GID and to stand against those who would abuse and harm human beings by teaching the very opposite of what we are, and what God has made us.

---

24. *When Harry Became Sally*, Ryan T. Anderson, Encounter Books, 2018.

CONSIDER: Why do you think Transgender philosophy has become so important to the leaders of our society? Why do people get so angry about it? What harm do you think it does to teach young children that they can choose and change their own gender? How do we love those who suffer from GID, but stand up against those who would impose anti-Christian and harmful teaching about gender upon society?

RECOMMENDED FURTHER READING:
Transgender – Vaughan Roberts
When Harry met Sally – Ryan T. Anderson

PRAYER: O Lord God Almighty, what a world we live in! You created it good and at the apex of that creation you created human beings – male and female. And then sin entered the world and everything was broken, including us. In today's world we think we can remake humanity. O Lord, stop us! Save us from our own foolishness. Do not leave us. And enable each of us to honour you with our bodies, to care for all your creation and to follow your ways, in Jesus' name. Amen.

37. LOVING YOURSELF

QUESTION: How can I feel better about myself? How can I love myself, so I can love others?

BIBLE READING: Leviticus 19:1-18

TEXT: Do not seek revenge or bear a grudge against anyone among your people, but love your neighbour as yourself. I am the LORD (Leviticus 19:18).

This is a big question that is obviously important to many people - which is why there are hundreds of books in print about how to feel better about yourself. You can search the Internet and find lots of answers. Most of them offer feel good advice. Take this one random example I have just read – in order to feel better about yourself you should: 1) figure out your needs, 2) live authentically, 3) forgive yourself and 4) celebrate your quirks. There you go – sorted. Except it's not – which is why there will be many more books, courses, therapies and solutions for those of us who struggle with how we think about ourselves.

The trouble is that some of us think far too highly of ourselves, and we cannot understand why everyone does not join in our self-praise. But many of us go the opposite direction and we have a degree of self-pity if not self-loathing. We cannot imagine that anyone would really like us because we don't really like ourselves. How can we have a better attitude to ourselves? What does the Bible say?

Turning to the book of Leviticus may not seem the obvious answer but starting with our verse for today we can see a way ahead. We are to love our neighbours as ourselves. Ah – but what if the problem is that we don't love ourselves? The trouble is the same as if we think too highly of ourselves.

'For by the grace given me I say to every one of you: Do not think of yourself more highly than you ought, but rather think of yourself with sober judgement, in accordance with the faith God has distributed to each of you' (Romans 12:3).

It's always about self. It's always about me. We are to think of ourselves in the light of something bigger. The difference between low self-esteem and high self-esteem is minimal. Both are wrong and both do a great deal of harm to others and ourselves.

The trick is to think of ourselves less. Which is very hard to do – unless we get the bigger picture. One part, as we can see by reading the verses in Leviticus chapter 19, is that we should consider the needs of others. Care for your family, look out for the poor, don't take others' goods, don't lie, take care of your neighbour, protect the disabled, don't slander, don't hate and don't take revenge. I don't think this passage is telling us

– wait until you love yourself and then you can love others. It's pointing out that one way to love ourselves is to care for others. We look after our own bodies so we ought also to look after the collective body.

But there is more. We are to be holy. We are to offer right worship. We are to remember who is the Lord. We can love others and we can love ourselves when we know the love of God. He is the source of all love.

We live in a society in the West where human beings and human life is being increasingly devalued. I know that many of our cultural leaders will deny this – but it is the fruit of their philosophies. If we are just a blob of carbon floating from one meaningless existence to another – then what ultimate value do we have? If there is no absolute right or wrong and each person just makes up their own – what value is that? If there is an unwanted baby in the womb, or an unwanted older person who we consider to have lost their value for society – then why not just get rid of them? If you feel useless and unloved, why not just take your own life?

But when you think of God. When you understand what Jesus thinks of you. When you grasp the immense value of every human life – including yours – then what a difference that makes.

'I praise you because I am fearfully and wonderfully made; your works are wonderful, I know that full well' (Psalm 139:14).

That gives you a whole different perspective.

Most of all when you come to know Jesus as your Lord and Saviour there is a wonderful change in your life – so that the centre of your life no longer becomes you, but him. As Paul tells the Galatians – it's only when we stop focusing on ourselves and realise that our life is Christ-centred not me-centred, that we are truly set free to live.

'*I have been crucified with Christ and I no longer live, but Christ lives in me. The life I now live in the body, I live by faith in the Son of God, who loved me and gave himself for me*' (Galatians 2:20).

CONSIDER: Why is it so hard to forget about ourselves? Why do we so often feel bad about ourselves? Can you see a solution in what we have looked at above? How would you encourage someone who was really discouraged about themselves? What difference does Jesus make?

RECOMMENDED FURTHER READING: *The Freedom of Self-Forgetfulness* – Tim Keller

PRAYER: Lord, I am fearfully and wonderfully made. But sometimes I don't feel that. The trouble is when I try to stop thinking about myself, I am thinking about myself and often I don't like what I see. Please give me a different perspective. Help me to see myself in Christ, forgiven and clothed in his righteousness, not my own self-righteous filthy rags. Help me to serve and love others because I have come to see how infinitely valuable every human being is, including me. Amen.

38. FEELING GOD IS FAR AWAY

QUESTION: Sometimes I feel that God is far away from my family? How can I strengthen my faith?

BIBLE READING: Psalm 13

TEXT: How long, LORD? Will you forget me forever?
How long will you hide your face from me?
How long must I wrestle with my thoughts
and day after day have sorrow in my heart?
How long will my enemy triumph over me?
(Psalm 13:1-2)

Often I feel that God is far away. There are times when I really sense his presence but many more times when that is not the case. The worst times are when I long for his presence, but although I know he hears and answers, yet I do not 'feel'. What are we to do in such circumstances?

This short psalm really helps us. David feels that God has forgotten him. He cannot see God's face – this was a way of expressing that he thought that God's favour was not upon him and that God had looked away from him. This caused him to wrestle with his thoughts and have sorrow in his heart. He felt that his enemy was triumphing over him. Things are not good for him – so what does he do?

He prays in verses 3-4. He takes every circumstance to the Lord. His doubts, his fears and what is happening to him. We don't just pray when we 'feel' close to God. Perhaps we need to pray all the more when we feel far away. But you will notice that he doesn't just pray for his own feelings, but he prays for God's glory. That is what really bothers him. There is also an element of despair in his prayer. Sometimes the Lord lets us come to an end of ourselves so that we will truly turn to him.

One of our great fears is that because of our feelings we think that the Lord has forgotten us. In that case we need to turn to the Word of God, and not our feelings. What does God say should be the question – not what do I feel.

> But Zion said, 'The LORD has forsaken me,
> the Lord has forgotten me.'
> 'Can a mother forget the baby at her breast
> and have no compassion on the child she has borne?
> Though she may forget,
> I will not forget you!' (Isaiah 49:14-15)

Keep your lives free from the love of money and be content with what you have, because God has said:
> '... Never will I leave you;never will I forsake you.'
> So we say with confidence, 'The Lord is my helper; I will not be afraid. What can mere mortals do to me?' (Hebrews 13:5-6)

The fact is that our hearts will often condemn us – but God is greater than our hearts. Paul for example felt that he was under great pressure and despaired even of life (2 Corinthians 1:8-9). But such trials are designed to bring us closer to God, not take us further away. Often what we thought were deep experiences of the presence of God were actually quite shallow. In order to go deeper sometimes God has to cut deep.

Recognising the problem – seeking the Lord's face – asking him if there is any blockage, any hidden sin within us – and looking to his Word rather than our feelings will eventually lead to what David experienced in verses five and six.

He praises – There is a transformation in attitude if not in circumstances. There is no indication that what had caused his despair and feeling far away was changed. But what changed was his perception and his focus. Now he trusts in God's unfailing love, not his feelings. It's not that the feelings are unimportant. He wants to feel close to God. It's just that he does not rely on, or begin with the feelings. He rejoices in God's salvation and he is then able to sing his praises. That is often the pattern.

For you and your family it is important to look to Christ and seek him as you find him in his Word. Pray, have fellowship with his people, and hold on in the dark hours. I have often found books such as the one I suggest below really helpful, because they take time to assess our hearts and gently lead us back into the presence of Christ.

CONSIDER: Why do you think you might feel far from the presence of God? What is the danger of relying on your feelings rather than the Word of God? How important are your feelings?

RECOMMENDED FURTHER READING:

The Bruised Reed – Richard Sibbes

PRAYER: How long, LORD? Will you forget me forever?
How long will you hide your face from me?
How long must I wrestle with my thoughts
and day after day have sorrow in my heart?
How long will my enemy triumph over me?
(Psalm 13:1-2)

39. THE TRINITY, PRAYER AND EXAMS

QUESTION: Who can I ask for help before an exam or any other situation? God the Father, the Son, or the Holy Spirit?

BIBLE READING: 1 Peter 5:8-11

TEXT: Cast all your anxiety on him because he cares for you (1 Peter 5:7)

It's great that you want to ask God for help. That is what we call prayer! It's also good that you are thinking about who we pray to. The disciples came to Jesus and asked him to teach them to pray – and that is how we got the Lord's Prayer. Let's think what prayer is.

There is a danger in using prayer in the way that someone uses a vending machine. You put your money in and out comes whatever you desire – a drink or chocolate. You need to make sure you put the right money into the right machine. Prayer is not like that. God is not at our beck and call. We need to be very careful not to treat prayer like a work in which if we do it right enough and long enough we get what we want. Prayer is first of all saying to God, 'Your will be done.' So let's look at the Lord's Prayer which is a pattern for us (Matthew 6:9-13) and see how we would pray it when we are facing an exam.

OUR FATHER IN HEAVEN – This is who we pray to. God the Father. The normal pattern in Christian prayer is to pray to the Father, through the Son, in the power of the Spirit. Of course we can and should pray to Jesus the Son and asking the Holy Spirit to come to us is not wrong but the primary focus is on our Father in heaven – who as Peter tells us, cares for us to the extent that we can cast all our anxiety on him.

HALLOWED BE YOUR NAME – We begin with God and we continue with God. The focus in prayer is not ourselves.

YOUR KINGDOM COME, YOUR WILL BE DONE ON EARTH AS IT IS IN HEAVEN – Again we continue with God. We are longing for his kingdom to come. We want his will, not ours to be done.

GIVE US TODAY OUR DAILY BREAD – Now we are on to our exams. Our daily bread refers not just to food but all the necessities of life. As a student/pupil passing exams is a big deal in your life so of course it is not wrong to ask God to help you. Although asking him to let you miraculously pass the exams when you have done no work for them might not be the best way to go! Asking for mercy is one thing – presuming

that you don't need to do the work because all you have to do
is pray and God will pass the exam for you is quite another! So
praying that God would calm our minds, that we would have a
good memory, that he would bless our work and enable us to
pass the exam is a good thing to pray.

**FORGIVE US OUR DEBTS AS WE ALSO HAVE FORGIVEN
OUR DEBTORS** – Now in prayer we are considering our own
sins, including our attitudes to others. We are to let go of all
bitterness and hatred and seek forgiveness from our own sins.
We know that if we confess our sins he is faithful and just and
will forgive us our sins (1 John 1:9). It may be at this stage that we
are aware of not having done our work and we are asking the
Lord to show us mercy in our exam! That we are really repentant
and want to ensure that we don't behave that way again!

**LEAD US NOT INTO TEMPTATION BUT DELIVER US FROM
EVIL** – There may be a temptation to panic, or despair, or even
to cheat. We ask the Lord to deliver us from these.

**FOR YOURS IS THE KINGDOM, THE POWER AND THE
GLORY, FOREVER AND EVER. AMEN** – We finish as we began
– with God and his kingdom. Ultimately our exams are tiny
and small in the great scheme of things – but they still matter
to us and to the one who loves and knows us in so much detail
that he even knows every single hair on our head. So we ask
the Father, through the Son, by the Spirit, that we may pass
our exams and we trust that whatever happens he loves us and
will take care of us – because we are part of his kingdom, part
of his family.

I should point out that this only applies if we are part of his family – if we have come to a living and saving faith in Jesus Christ. If you are not a Christian please don't think you can use God at your own convenience to get what you want. Your greatest need is not passing exams but giving your life to Christ. The greatest question you will ever answer is, 'What do you think of Christ?'

CONSIDER: What does Jesus tell us to do about worry? What are the things you worry about? How do you cast all your anxiety (worry) upon him? Do you just pray when you feel a need or is prayer part of your DNA?

RECOMMENDED FURTHER READING:
Prayer – Experiencing Awe and Intimacy with God – Tim Keller
The Valley of Vision – Arthur G. Bennett

PRAYER: Lord, teach us to pray. Teach us who you are. Teach us who we are. May your kingdom come. Amen.

40. WHY PRAY?

Question: Why pray about things if God has already planned what is going to happen? What is the point?

BIBLE READING: James 5:13-20

TEXT: The prayer of a righteous person is powerful and effective (James 5:16:b).

There is a great deal of confusion and misunderstanding about this question. It misunderstands prayer, God and ourselves. If prayer is seeking to persuade God to do something that he doesn't want to do – as though we are arguing and negotiating with someone who doesn't know what is going on – then yes – this would be a problem. But that is clearly not the case. God is all-knowing. We pray from our heart and God knows what is already on our heart.

So what is the point? Why don't we have a fatalistic view and say 'que sera, sera ... whatever will be, will be' and just accept our fate? Because God in his sovereignty has made us in his image and has made us moral creatures with the responsibility to choose good and to choose to serve him. He has also determined to work through his people and especially through their prayers.

Fatalism is not a Christian attribute. In fact it is the very opposite. Buddhism and Islam are largely fatalistic – as is much of modern society. Genetic determinism is the view that our genes (as well as our environment) so determine us that we do not really have any free will. They argue that we feel as though we have, but in reality we don't. Whereas the Christian perspective is almost the opposite – sometimes we feel as if everything is meaningless and pointless because there is nothing we can do. But God has ordained in his sovereignty a means whereby we can be both free and impact and change things. Prayer is the key to that.

James tells us what to do when we are sick and when we are overwhelmed by sin. He doesn't say, 'there is nothing you can do, just sit back and accept your fate'. Instead he urges us to bring in the elders of the church and to get them to pray and anoint with oil (a symbol of the Holy Spirit). He gives the example of Elijah who prayed 'earnestly' and whose prayers were answered.

There is a balance that we need to get right here. On the one hand some so stress the sovereignty of God and the fact that we can do nothing without him that they see no point in praying. On the other, there are those who think that prayer is a work which depends entirely on them and they think that if only they have the right technique, the right feelings and they put in enough effort then God is bound to reward them with the answers they want.

A much more balanced and Christian perspective is to pray to a Sovereign God who in his sovereignty has asked us to pray and has promised that he hears the prayers of his people. It is always the devil's aim to get us not to pray, or when we pray to ask with wrong motives or with a wrong view of God.

It's a great idea when you read the Bible, that every time you notice a promise from God – you write it down. Pray the promises. If God has promised something and you pray for it, then you know that you are praying in accordance with his will.

'Which of you, if your son asks for bread, will give him a stone? Or if he asks for a fish, will give him a snake? If you, then, though you are evil, know how to give good gifts to your children, how much more will your Father in heaven give good gifts to those who ask him!' (Matthew 7:9-11).

But we need to ask. And we need to ask trusting in our good and gracious God to give what is best for us, and what will most bring glory to his name.

Why pray? Because Jesus did. And he asks us to. And we claim to be his followers. Do we need any other reason?

CONSIDER: Why do you think the fact that God is sovereign should inspire you to pray, rather than stop you praying? What is your prayer life like? Do you keep a prayer diary? Do you ever use books of prayers or the prayers of the Bible, especially the psalms?

RECOMMENDED FURTHER READING:
If God Already Knows – Why Pray? – Douglas F. Kelly
How Prayer Impacts Lives – Ed. Catherine Mackenzie

PRAYER: LORD, hear my prayer,
   listen to my cry for mercy;
   in your faithfulness and righteousness
   come to my relief (Psalm 143:1).

41. WORRY

QUESTION: The Bible says do not be anxious about anything, but what if you struggle with anxiety? How do we take this verse then? Is it a sin to have anxiety?

BIBLE READING: Matthew 6:24-34

TEXT: But seek first his kingdom and his righteousness, and all these things will be given to you as well. Therefore do not worry about tomorrow, for tomorrow will worry about itself. Each day has enough trouble of its own (Matthew 6:33-34).

It's best to look at this chapter together with chapters 39 and 40. Jesus says do not worry. And we then worry about worrying! That's the kind of mess we get ourselves into. So let's think about this carefully.

Note the last word of that last sentence. Is Jesus saying we are not to care about anything? Of course not! We are to be a people who care. But when does care move over into worry and an anxiety that is sinful and wrong? I think the clue is in the context of the passage – remember, as we have seen several times already in this book, we are never to take Bible verses out of context – because then we almost inevitably will misunderstand them.

In the *Sermon on the Mount*, Jesus is not saying don't ever be concerned or anxious about anything. Jesus himself was concerned. For example when he was in the Garden of Gethsemane he agonized over going to the cross.

'And being in anguish, he prayed more earnestly, and his sweat was like drops of blood falling to the ground' (Luke 22:44).

He didn't just saunter up to the cross saying 'no worries'!

What he was concerned with in our text are those who are anxious and worried about the wrong things. They are seeking first the things of this world. They fear losing their income more than they fear losing their God.

In one way what Jesus says is not very encouraging – every day has enough trouble of its own! *Every* day will have more than enough trouble for us, but what he is saying is that we can trust our heavenly Father to provide for all our needs. He has just taught us to pray 'give us today our daily bread'. This is what that means practically. God usually won't give you a big store of things to last well into the future (although it is not wrong to save) but he will provide for you on a daily basis. I think one of the reasons for this is that we learn to come to him on a daily basis. My mother-in-law was brought up on the Scottish Isle of Lewis where in the 1930s there were really hard times for many ordinary people. She told me once that then when they sat down to pray 'give us today our daily bread', they meant it, because they were not sure where their daily food was going to come from. Now we rely on 24/7 supermarkets, freezers and all the mod cons of life that enable us to forget that the food chain is still fragile. One computer attack could do a whole lot more damage in one sense than a nuclear bomb (and that's not an excuse for you to start worrying about either of those!). The point is that we are to seek daily provision from a gracious Father. If we believe that that is what he is – then we will not have the kind of anxiety and cares that cripple us.

Because we pray – as Paul tells the Philippians:

'Do not be anxious about anything, but in every situation, by prayer and petition, with thanksgiving, present your requests to God (Philippians 4:6).

That is how we deal with anxiety and worry. We present our requests to God and we leave them at the throne of grace.

One problem I have with this question is that it seems to have a view of God that is harsh, cruel and capricious. It's as though Jesus is mocking us … 'don't be anxious, because if you are it's a great sin', which will then make a naturally anxious person, even more anxious! It will greatly help us if we learn to stop looking in at ourselves and instead look up to our God. Sometimes there are those in our lives who help take away our anxiety – a loving, strong father holding the hand of their fearful child; a mother bringing comfort through a hug; a friend who sticks closer than a brother. I hope you have people like that in your life. But the real friend who sticks closer than a brother is of course Jesus.

What a friend we have in Jesus,
All our sins and griefs to bear.
What a privilege to carry,
Everything to God in prayer.
O what peace we often forfeit,

O what needless pain we bear.
All because we do not carry,
Everything to God in prayer.[25]

CONSIDER: What is the difference between care and worrying? When do you think worrying might become sinful? If you are a naturally anxious person how do you think that can be helped? Do you think there are times when we don't worry and we should?

RECOMMENDED FURTHER READING:
Anxious for Nothing – John Macarthur

PRAYER: Our Father in heaven, when anxiety was great within me, your consolation brought me joy (Psalm 94:19). You are good and the giver of all things good. You tell us when we are weary and heavy-laden to come to you and you will give us rest. O Lord I come to you now and ask that the peace of Christ which passes all understanding, will be mine. In Jesus' name. Amen.

---

25. *What a Friend we have in Jesus*, Joseph M. Scriven, 1855.

42. CHRISTIAN COMMUNITY AND THE INTERNET

QUESTION: We are an Internet generation and spend a lot of our time on the Internet. How can we build Christian community that upholds Christian values and not become foreign to our own families and churches?

BIBLE READING: Hebrews 10:19-25

TEXT: And let us consider how we may spur one another on toward love and good deeds not giving up meeting together, as some are in the habit of doing, but encouraging one another—and all the more as you see the Day approaching (Hebrews 10:24-25).

The Internet is a massive development which Christians need to think about; as important in the twenty-first century as the invention of the printing press was in the sixteenth. So thank you for your question that highlights one very important aspect – how does it impact upon our building Christian community?

I am writing this in Sydney where every day I take the train into Moore College. Every day the story is the same – the train is filled with people glued to their phones. Maybe people never did talk on trains, but they certainly don't now. Even at sporting events, the cinema and church, people are often on their phone.

I find my phone and laptop – through which I access the Internet – to be a great boon to life. I have maps, radio, music, sermons, talks, address books, actual books, articles, praise and so much more. I can easily 'find' my family and through the wonders of Skype and social media speak to friends and family in almost every country in the world. It's a great gift. And it's a great curse.

The Internet gives us lots of information, but it doesn't give us wisdom. It provides us with entertainment but at such a level that we are far too easily distracted. Tony Reinke in our recommended book cites the philosopher Douglas Groothuis who says, 'It is difficult to serve God with our heart, soul, strength and mind when we are diverted and distracted and multi-tasking everything'; and Bruce Hindmarsh who adds, 'Our spiritual condition today is one of spiritual ADD'.

The big issue in terms of our question is that the Internet is supposed to connect us with the whole world. But in reality it ends up disconnecting us from those around us. Just sit in a restaurant and watch a family who are supposed to be having a nice night out together – how often are they just staring at their phones? Personal confession time – I think that I am someone who has become so addicted to my phone that it makes me rude and disconnects me from people and the world around. How can it be otherwise if you are constantly walking around with your buds in your ear and your eyes on your screen?

We need to build community. We need family and friends. And we need to ensure that our church communities are a great place to be friends and family. The Internet can be a tool to help us with that, but we always need to remember that it is a great servant but a terrible master.

In terms of church community – we don't need 'internet church' just as we don't need Facebook friends. I have over 10,000 'friends' on social media – but they are not real friends. I don't know the vast majority of them. We don't need those kind of friends – we need real ones. We also don't need followers – we need to follow Christ.

Knowing how to build a Christian community that upholds Christian values, as the family of God is not that difficult. The Bible tells us. We need the Word of God (the Bible), prayer and meeting together as we share in the fellowship of the Father, the Son and the Holy Spirit. As we meet together we encourage one another. That is why the church is so important. You don't get to self-select your friends in church – every believer is your brother and sister. We can't just 'defriend' them – we are obliged to love them – and they us.

It is little wonder that there is so little Christian community when we think that church is something that we go to for one hour per week, rather than something that we are all the time. This is not an excuse to stay away from the public gathering of the Lord's people and public worship, but rather a reason to go all the more. Every time you gather with God's people to hear God's Word, to sing his praises and to pray with and for his people, you are encouraging and building Christian community. Every time you stay away you are discouraging and de-constructing that community that you so long for.

CONSIDER: How much time do you spend on the Internet? How much time do you spend on your phone/computer? Is there an addiction problem? How do you think that can be cured? What are the ways that you think you could help build Christian community?

RECOMMENDED FURTHER READING:
12 Ways Your Phone is Changing You – Tony Reinke

PRAYER: O Lord, we thank you for the gift of the Internet and all the joy and opportunities it brings. But we confess, as with all things, that we are so prone to take what is good and use it for something evil. We pray that our linking to the 'world wide web' would not take us away from the community of your people. Help us to be faithful members of a local church and to serve and build up your body there, for your glory. Amen.

43. COOL CHRISTIANITY

QUESTION: How can I be cool and still a Christian?

BIBLE READING: 1 Corinthians 1:18-31

TEXT: For the message of the cross is foolishness to those who are perishing, but to us who are being saved it is the power of God (1 Corinthians 1:18).

Why would you want to be cool? I guess it depends what it means. In Western culture it has come to mean someone who is considered fashionable, in touch, someone you want to hang out with. To be the 'cool' kid in the class is the ultimate aim for some. You dress cool, you talk cool, you look cool, you have cool taste in music and your girlfriend/boyfriend is cool (somewhat confusingly they need to be 'hot' to be cool!). There is an old sit-com on the TV called 'Happy Days' in which a group of American young people hung around in a café, cars and other cool places. The ultimate in cool, and the one they all aspired to be like was 'the Fonz' (having a cool nickname is also necessary). Occasionally he would go to the mirror pull out a comb and then put it back commenting how perfect his carefully coiffured hair was. Nowadays I suspect even the Fonz would no longer be considered as cool.

In those terms being a Christian is not usually regarded as the ultimate in cool! Why? Again it all has to do with image – Christians are perceived as out of date, old-fashioned, irrelevant and somewhat weird. We are about as cool as a woollen suit on the beach. This does create a difficulty for some young Christians – can we have Christ and be cool? Well – yes – but only as an incidental and not as something that we aim for.

A few years ago a young student from our church who was definitely on the cool end of the spectrum, told me; 'David, you are so uncool it's cool!' I think it was intended as a compliment!

The whole problem here is when we allow the fashions of this world to determine and shape who we are. It is almost always false. It's about image and style, not reality and substance. As Christians we believe and do things – not because they are cool, but because we want to be like Christ.

There is a verse in the Bible that does mention 'hot' and 'cold'.

'To the angel of the church in Laodicea write: These are the words of the Amen, the faithful and true witness, the ruler of God's creation. I know your deeds, that you are neither cold nor hot. I wish you were either one or the other! So, because you are lukewarm— neither hot nor cold—I am about to spit you out of my mouth' (Revelation 3:14-16).

Jesus was so concerned that about the lukewarmness of some of his professing people that he warned them they made him feel ill. They were not hostile to him, but their first love had been lost. The passion and the fire had gone.

Rather than being concerned as to how cool we are in the eyes of the world, we should be asking how hot we are in our love for Jesus and what are we doing about it?

To the world the preaching of the cross is foolishness. The cross of Jesus is the ultimate in uncool. He was supposed to be the Messiah and he ended up dying the worst of deaths, with his disciples having deserted him and his own people having rejected him. What a loser! And yet the foolishness of men is the wisdom of God. Christ is the ultimate wisdom. I don't want to be associated with those who hate and despise the most beautiful and glorious person in history. All the idols that are considered cool today will be dust tomorrow and forgotten the day after. But Jesus lives and reigns forever.

Ultimately every one of us faces a choice. Are we going to follow the King of kings and Lord of lords, or are we going to give that up for a brief taste of being considered cool by those around us. We need to be like Moses – who refused to be known as the son of Pharaoh's daughter (which would have been really cool in his culture) but:

'He chose to be mistreated along with the people of God rather than to enjoy the fleeting pleasures of sin. He regarded disgrace for the sake of Christ as of greater value than the treasures of Egypt, because he was looking ahead to his reward' (Hebrews 11:25-26).

Of course being a Christian does not mean that you have to deliberately go against the fashions of this world and try to make yourself as uncool as possible. That is to make the same mistake as those who seek to be cool – judging by outward appearances. Look to Christ – and everything else will take care of itself!

Finally remember that Christ came for all, the uncool as well as the cool. Make sure that you never despise people because they are not as hip and happening as you. All are human beings made in the image of God.

CONSIDER: Why do people want to be cool? What do you think cool is? Do you think we can overreact against this? How would you reach 'cool' people with the gospel? What about those who are considered 'uncool'?

RECOMMENDED FURTHER READING:
The Holiness of God – R.C. Sproul

PRAYER: Our Father, we bless you that our value does not depend on image and the perception of others. We thank you that when we come to you through your Son Jesus, we are clothed in his beauty and you value us as your children. Help us to continually seek our value and worth in you, and help us to value all human beings, however the rest of society regards them. Amen.

44. BACKSLIDING

QUESTION: I keep on backsliding as a Christian and have to confess again and again – What can I do so I confess once and for all and stop backsliding?

BIBLE READING: 1 John 1

TEXT: If we confess our sins, he is faithful and just and will forgive us our sins and purify us from all unrighteousness'(1 John 1:9).

Thanks for this question – it's one that has appeared in various forms (have a look at questions 17, 19 and 34) – but we need to look at it because it is so important. The devil is the accuser of the brothers and sisters so he wants to ensure that we are defeated and kept down by his accusations.

How do people get caught up in a habitual sin (sexual, financial, gluttony, drunkenness or many others)? The pattern is often that we first of all do something that is wrong and are utterly horrified and thoroughly repentant. Then a while later we do it again. This time we are not quite so horrified and the repentance doesn't last so long. The next time it is even less and shorter.

I think of the student who would come to see me on a Sunday night, thoroughly penitent because of his actions in the student union the previous night. We would talk and pray together. But the same thing would happen the next Sunday and the one after that. What was going on? The truth is that he was doing something that he knew was wrong....and every time he did it he felt bad afterwards. But what he felt was remorse not repentance. How do we know that? Real repentance is changed behaviour.

Let's just go a little deeper as we consider what real repentance is. The Shorter Catechism asks in question 87: What is repentance unto life? And answers, 'Repentance unto life is a saving grace, whereby a sinner, out of a true sense of his sin, and apprehension of the mercy of God in Christ, doth, with grief and hatred of his sin, turn from it unto God, with full purpose of, and endeavour after, new obedience.' Forget the old fashioned language and instead let's just unpack this.

Repentance is something that comes from God. So instead of trying to work it up, maybe we need to ask God to show us our sin and cause us to see it as he does? That will then give us a true sense of our sin that would overwhelm us if it were not for our 'apprehension of the mercy of God in Christ'. We need a genuine awareness not only of our sin but also of the incredible mercy of God in Christ. Both those things combined cause us to hate and grieve for our sin (it is something which nailed Christ to the tree – it was my sin that held him there – and something which does harm to us, those around us and God's world). Not only to hate and grieve but also to turn.

This is what repentance is – a turning *away* from sin and a turning *to* God. The trouble for many of us is that we try to turn away from sin but we turn in on ourselves. There is no solution in us. When we turn to God and in the words of our text confess our sin and ask him to forgive us, the difference between remorse and real repentance, is that there is a full intention to newly obey God and an endeavour to do so.

By the way you will never confess 'once and for all' and never sin again. As Martin Luther pointed out, the Christian life is one of continual daily repentance. But the difference between the 'repentance unto life' and the remorse you are describing is that whilst the latter has no power except to pile on the guilt, the former renews, cleanses and restores us. Every time I sit at the Lord's table and take communion it is a reminder for me of what Christ has done – how he confessed once for all – how his atoning sacrifice really does atone. It is always a time of renewal and new beginning.

So please – stop focusing on yourself and your sin. Look to Christ. 'For every look at self, take ten looks at Christ.'[26] It will break your heart to realise what you are doing to him by sinning – and that will be enough to cause you to truly repent and endeavour after new obedience.

CONSIDER: How do you break out of the cycle of despair caused by habitual sin? Why is it important to look more at Jesus than at ourselves? Do you think it is helpful to realise that we can never defeat our own sin, but we can look to the one who cleanses and renews from all sin?

---

26. *Unfathomable Oceans of Grace*, Robert Murray McCheyne (1813-1843), Letter, 1840.

RECOMMENDED FURTHER READING:
Indwelling Sin in Believers (abridged and made easy to read) –
John Owen

PRAYER: O my God, have mercy on me
in your steadfast love, I pray;
In your infinite compassion
my transgressions wipe away.
Cleanse me from iniquity;
wash my sin away from me.

Lord, create a pure heart in me,
and a steadfast mind renew.
Do not take your Spirit from me;
cast me not away from you.
Give me back the joy I had;
keep my willing spirit glad.
(Psalm 51:1-2, 10-12 – *Sing Psalms*[27])

---

27. *Sing Psalms*, Free Church of Scotland, 2003.

45. HELP – MY GIRLFRIEND'S PREGNANT

QUESTION: I got my girlfriend pregnant, she's not a believer what do I/we do?
I am pregnant and terrified to tell my strict Christian parents. What do I do?

BIBLE READING: John 8:1-15

TEXT: Jesus straightened up and asked her, 'Woman, where are they? Has no one condemned you?' 'No one, sir,' she said. 'Then neither do I condemn you,' Jesus declared. 'Go now and leave your life of sin' (John 8:10-11).

Both these situations are a mess. And there is no quick fix or simple solution. Whatever happens there is going to be pain and trouble. But there is no need to despair because Christ came to deliver us from our sins and he is there to help – just as he was to help the woman who was caught in adultery and was about to be punished.

There are several ways that people try to deal with this kind of situation. Some attempt to cover it up – that is really difficult and would be a mistake to even attempt. Others want to make light of the situation and treat it as a bit of a joke – which as I am sure you are aware it is anything but.

Then there are those who attempt the quick fix. Let me tell you about one young man who came to me a number of years ago. He was deeply concerned because his teenage girlfriend was pregnant. He was not a Christian, but his girlfriend had, as you put it, 'strict Christian parents'. She was too scared to tell them and as a result was going to have an abortion. We went and spoke to her. She was terrified about what they would think and was also ashamed that she had let them down. What could be done? The answer of the social worker was to have an abortion. But we know, and his girlfriend knew, that abortion is the taking of a human life. So we went with her parents' minister to speak to them. Rather than the condemnation she expected – instead they loved and supported her. Of course they were not happy about the situation, but neither were they going to abandon their daughter. Their response was very much the Christian one. Perhaps not every parent will behave like that but whatever the case we have no right to take the life of the unborn child.

The only real option each person has is to face up to the facts as they are, to come to terms with them and to make the best out of a bad situation. That will involve confession and repentance to God and to all who are involved. There will be hurt but there can also be healing. If you are a Christian then clearly you have not been walking with the Lord. His teaching about sex before marriage is very clear and you have gone against that. But this is not the unforgivable sin. Don't excuse it but don't despair either. You will now have responsibility for another precious human life. You will need help and support – seek it from your family, church, school and other agencies.

If you are not a Christian then the most important thing is that you become one. Not only do you need forgiveness but also you need the support and help of Christ to face the life ahead. Like the woman in our text, if you are to go and 'leave your life of sin', you will need him to be with you.

I don't know you, but even as I write I am praying for you ... that you will know the Lord's peace, forgiveness, healing and guidance as you face the future. God is able to turn even this ugly mess into something beautiful.

CONSIDER: What are the best ways to prevent us getting into these types of situations? How would you help a friend who was facing similar circumstances? Why do you think that people think abortion is a simple solution? What is wrong with abortion?

RECOMMENDED FURTHER READING:

Life Interrupted: The Scoop on Being a Young Mom – Tricia Goyer

PRAYER: Father in heaven, I confess that I have sinned. I can see my life is in such a mess, and because of that other people's lives are messed up as well. I come to you seeking your forgiveness and asking you to renew me. To create a clean heart within me, and to grant me pure hands. Help me to serve and honour you as I face up to the reality of what I have done and grant that you would bring great good out of the mess I have created, in your name. Amen.

46. TATTOOS AND ALCOHOL

QUESTION: Is it a sin to get tattooed? Can I get a tattoo of my favourite Bible verse? Is it ok to drink alcohol? How do we know what's right and wrong?

BIBLE READING: 1 Corinthians 6:12-20

TEXT: Do you not know that your bodies are temples of the Holy Spirit, who is in you, whom you have received from God? You are not your own; you were bought at a price. Therefore honour God with your bodies (1 Corinthians 6:19-20).

If you have been reading through this book you will have become familiar with our text for this question! So many questions we have as teenagers are to do with our bodies so it is not surprising that this verse, which states a major guiding principle, is used so much. Maybe it would be a good idea to have it as one of your verses to memorise? (I hope you do memorise the Word of God and store it up in your heart). It's also essential to realise that the Bible is not a list of do's and don'ts – it's not a moral checklist. Rather it gives us Christ and it gives us the principles on which we can base our life. The Bible treats us like responsible adults who have the capacity to think for ourselves and to work out God's Word in our local circumstances. So with that in mind let's look briefly at the two issues mentioned in our questions.

Is it a sin to have a tattoo? At first glance the answer seems to be an obvious yes. After all doesn't Leviticus 19:28 say:

'Do not cut your bodies for the dead or put tattoo marks on yourselves. I am the LORD.'

But that is the danger with taking a cut and paste verse approach to the Bible – remember the principle that we have stated several times – everything must be taken in context. Is this like the verse afterwards which tells fathers not to make their daughters prostitutes or the one before which tells them not to cut their hair at the sides or trim their beards?! Are we going to say that all of them apply equally today or that none of them apply? It seems to me that neither of these options are biblical.

In the context of the Levitical law and culture of that day, the shaping of the hair and trimming of beards, as well as tattooing patterns on the skin, were part of pagan mourning practice. God is saying don't mourn like pagans. Tattoos were often of pagan deities and were considered to be a dishonouring of the image of God in a person. (Deuteronomy 14:1-2). Neither of these practices were acceptable to the covenant people of God, who were to be separate/holy. So what about tattoos today? I don't think it is sinful to get a tattoo per se. It all depends what kind of tattoo and what the motive is. Interesting side fact: Ronaldo, the Real Madrid world cup star, does not have a tattoo because he wants to be able to give blood! I also think we need to be aware of the cultural context. Why are tattoos so popular today? Is it because as a society we are reverting to a pagan view of the body? If so, Christians need to be even more careful not to reflect that.

What about drinking alcohol? Psalm 104:15 thanks God for *'wine that gladdens human hearts'.* Jesus turned water into high quality wine (John 2:1-10). The memorial feast he established (communion) had wine as one of its two major elements. Paul, inspired by the Holy Spirit, tells Timothy to stop drinking just water and take a little wine for his stomach's sake (1 Timothy 5:23).

On the other hand there are strong warnings in the Bible against drunkenness – and we are commanded not to get drunk on wine which leads to debauchery but to be filled with the Holy Spirit (Ephesians 5:18). The Bible's position is, then, that alcohol is a gift from God, but it should be used properly and not to excess. What does this mean for us? We are free to drink alcohol and we are free not to. Another very important factor is to consider those around us. If you have a friend who is an alcoholic it would be unwise to drink in their presence. If there are those of our friends and family who abuse alcohol you don't want to encourage them. But please remember not to judge others for doing something that the Bible does not condemn.

How do we know what is right and wrong on these and other issues? Sometimes our conscience, sometimes our culture, but always the Word of God. Consciences can be seared and cultures can be corrupted – but the Word of God remains pure for all generations. We should not do what he has forbidden or refuse to do what he has commanded. There is a great liberty in understanding and applying this.

In all of this our desire is to show our love for God by obeying his commands (1 John 5:3). We follow Jesus. In this respect Revelation 19:16 has an interesting word about a 'tattoo' on Jesus:

'On his robe and on his thigh he has this name written: KING OF KINGS AND LORD OF LORDS.'

He is King of kings and Lord of lords. Follow Jesus and you won't get lost or wander into the wilderness.

CONSIDER: Why do you think God has not given a detailed set of rules for every situation?

RECOMMENDED FURTHER READING:
Principles of Conduct: Aspects of Biblical Ethics – John Murray
Knowing God's Will – M. Blaine Smith

PRAYER: How can a young person stay on the path of purity?
By living according to your word.
I seek you with all my heart;
do not let me stray from your commands.
I have hidden your word in my heart
that I might not sin against you.
Praise be to you, LORD;
teach me your decrees (Psalm 119:9-12).

47. BUDDHIST PARENTS

QUESTION: My parents are Buddhist, should I still obey them?

BIBLE READING: Mark 7:1-13

TEXT: For Moses said, 'Honour your father and mother,' and, 'Anyone who curses their father or mother is to be put to death.' But you say that if anyone declares that what might have been used to help their father or mother is Corban (that is, devoted to God)—then you no longer let them do anything for their father or mother. Thus you nullify the word of God by your tradition that you have handed down. And you do many things like that (Mark 7:10-13).

A young boy went home from a children's holiday club and when his mother asked him to do the dishes, shouted at her and told her that he didn't have to do that any more because he had become a Christian! Cue irate phone call from the mother to yours truly and a quick visit to the home to inform our young friend that he clearly had not become a Christian. By their fruits you shall know them.

When we become Christians we should become better children to our parents. We should honour and respect them even more than we did before. In the example given above the Pharisees were using the excuse of religion not to provide for their parents. We have a responsibility to provide for and care for our parents – especially as they get older. Your parents may be afraid that because you are a Christian you will honour them less. Show them that the opposite is the case.

However, if your parents ask you to do things that go directly against the Word of God that is a different matter. We are to honour and obey our parents – whatever their religion. But we are never to obey our parents absolutely. Let's take an extreme example – if your parents commanded you to go out and kill the next door neighbours' children, are you expected to do so?! Paul tells the Ephesians,

'Children, obey your parents in the Lord, for this is right.' (Ephesians 6:1).

We are to obey our parents *in the Lord*. Jesus put it strongly:

'If anyone comes to me and does not hate father and mother, wife and children, brothers and sisters—yes, even their own life— such a person cannot be my disciple' (Luke 14:26).

Obviously he did not mean that we are to hate our father and mother as a matter of course, any more than he meant we are not to love our own life! He is just simply saying that unless we are prepared to give up all those things we value most dearly, including our parents, we cannot be his disciples.

What if your parents want you to go to a Buddhist temple? I would suggest that it depends upon what age you are. A young child does not really have an option – but an older one does. Perhaps the story of Naaman might be helpful.

Naaman was commander of the king of Aram. When he was healed from his leprosy through Elisha (see 2 Kings 5 for the whole story) he promised not to worship any other God but the LORD.

'If you will not,' said Naaman, 'please let me, your servant, be given as much earth as a pair of mules can carry, for your servant will never again make burnt offerings and sacrifices to any other god but the LORD. But may the LORD forgive your servant for this one thing: When my master enters the temple of Rimmon to bow down and he is leaning on my arm and I have to bow there also—when I bow down in the temple of Rimmon, may the LORD forgive your servant for this.'

'Go in peace,' Elisha said (2 Kings 5:17-19).

He was asking for a special dispensation, when as part of his duties to his master he had to go into the temple of a pagan god and bow down with his master. He was given that dispensation. Again we have to be careful here – but I think there is a clear principle – that sometimes we are in situations where we are faced with the choice of two wrongs – in this case the wrong of being in a pagan temple vs. the wrong of disobeying his master. In this case Naaman was given permission to choose the former. On the other hand Daniel refused to go along with the commands to worship a pagan god.

These are difficult situations. They are part of the division that the gospel brings – but we hope and pray that they will also result in a greater unity – as your parents see that you love them more because you are a Christian, not less. Honour, respect, obey in the Lord and pray for them. God often works in families. May you be the messenger of salvation to them.

CONSIDER: Can you think of other situations where there might be a clash between our family/civic duties and our obedience to Christ? How can we have a loving disobedience?

RECOMMENDED FURTHER READING:
The Ten Commandments – J. Douma

PRAYER: Father in heaven, we bless you for our parents. Help us to honour, respect and love them. Help us never to put them before you, but may we glorify you by serving them, when such service is not against your will. Forgive us when we even use our faith in you to dishonour them. We pray that all we love would come to know you, in Jesus' name and for his glory. Amen.

48. MENTAL ILLNESS

QUESTION: What should be a Christian response to mental illness such as anxiety disorders, bipolar, schizophrenia etc.? How should Christians react, not only as personal sufferers but also how should we react to those in our community who have mental illness (both Christian and non-Christian)?

BIBLE READING: Isaiah 42:1-17

TEXT: A bruised reed he will not break,
and a smouldering wick he will not snuff out (Isaiah 42:3).

This is another question that is increasingly asked by teenagers. I suspect because there is a growing awareness of mental health issues. It may also be the case that because of various societal factors there is an actual increase in those who suffer from serious mental health problems. Around one in four adults will experience real mental health issues in their lifetime. By mental health issues we do not mean just the normal feeling blue, or forgetfulness or other emotional and mental factors. We use it to mean issues that affect the mind which end up being debilitating to such an extent that they can change and harm our lifestyles. As the dictionary puts it: 'A condition which causes serious disorder in a person's behaviour or thinking'.

Some Christians have a particular difficulty with experiencing and dealing with mental health illness. They don't recognize it as an illness. Although they would accept that Christians can get physically sick, they seem to think that Christians should not get mentally ill. But they seem to forget that all human beings, since the Fall, are living in a broken world, with decaying bodies, trapped wills and disturbed minds. There is no more reason for a Christian to think they will never experience mental illness than there is to think that we will never get sick.

Is it wrong for a Christian to get depressed? Isn't the joy of the Lord supposed to be our strength? How can we sing about peace and joy if at the same time we are feeling so depressed? Does that not indicate something wrong with our Christianity? Not at all. Not unless you want to dismiss the Bible. Jesus was overcome with sorrow, Paul knew what it was to struggle against the 'fightings within', and we even have a book of songs (the Psalms) that frequently express the deepest sorrow, angst and fears. When I asked a student why she came to our church she said, 'Because you let me be depressed'. I joked, 'That's a great advertising slogan – The Free Church – the church that let's you be depressed'. But rightly she rebuked me and said, 'I'm serious. I suffer from depression and it's dreadful when you go to a church and they try to cast out the demons or worse, cheer you up! I was just so happy to come here and you let me be depressed and even let me sing songs about it'. She was of course referring to the Psalms.

What can we do to help? Accepting the fact of mental illness does not mean that we do nothing – or we are just stoical about it. We will do what we can to avail ourselves of help and to help those who are struggling. Mental illness hits teenagers in many different forms. Eating disorders, depression, bi-polar, personality disorders amongst others. We should make use of the medical help and professionals that we have available. However we also have two great advantages that others do not have.

Firstly we have the church. Our churches should be places where the mentally ill are welcome and where they find and receive support. The community of the Lord's people can be a great help. We should follow the example of Jesus Christ in his strong, kind gentleness. The bruised reed he does not break. The smouldering wick he does not snuff out. Churches should be refuges, places of healing which offer hope, peace and restoration – whether in this life or in the life to come.

Then we have the great advantage of prayer. We come to one who was broken for us – who was tempted in every way just as we are.

'He heals the brokenhearted and binds up their wounds' (Psalm 147:3).

A Scottish theologian from the nineteenth century, 'Rabbi Duncan', put it beautifully: 'There is no pit so deep that Christ has not gone deeper still'.[28] One of the greatest problems we

---

28. Attributed to Rabbi Duncan.

have when we suffer from mental illness is that we feel we are alone, and that well meaning as they are, others cannot understand our situation because they have not experienced it. Christ has.

One other thought – if mental illness is 'a condition which causes serious disorder in a person's behaviour or thinking' is there not a sense in which all of us suffer to some degree from mental illness? Whilst it is not technically mental illness, it is nonetheless the case that sin has caused disorder in every single person's behaviour and thinking. We all need to be renewed in our minds and healed in our spirits.

CONSIDER: What is mental illness? Do you think it is wrong to seek help from mental health professionals? How do you think the Church can help those who suffer from mental illness?

RECOMMENDED FURTHER READING:
Dealing with Depression – Sarah Collins and Jane Haynes
The Big Ego Trip – Glenn Harrison
Eating Disorders – Emma Scrivener

PRAYER: Lord, I thank you that you are my shepherd. Even though I walk through the darkest valley, I will fear no evil, for you are with me; your rod and your staff, they comfort me (Psalm 23:4).

I thank you that you are close to the brokenhearted and save those who are crushed in spirit (Psalm 34:18). O Lord deliver us from evil. Restore, renew and heal. In the name of Jesus. Amen.

49. THE ROLE OF THE LAW

QUESTION: What is the role of the law in my life?

BIBLE READING: Galatians 3:1-14

TEXT: For all who rely on the works of the law are under a curse, as it is written: 'Cursed is everyone who does not continue to do everything written in the Book of the Law.' Clearly no one who relies on the law is justified before God, because 'the righteous will live by faith' (Galatians 3:10-11).

There have been many, many books and articles written about the role of the law in the Christian life. It seems as though spiritual lawyers like arguing about the law. Is this because the Bible is unclear? No – it's because there are great depths in the Bible and sometimes there is great potential for misunderstanding – not least because we are sinners who struggle with these issues, because they affect every one of us.

The first difficulty is when we ask – what do we mean by the term 'the Law'? Sometimes it can be used for the whole revealed Word of God. Sometimes Paul uses the word 'law' in general to refer to a principle or rule. Most often in the New Testament it is used of the Old Testament and especially the first five books of Moses known as the Pentateuch. It is a body of commands that are summarized in these books that came at a particular time in history.

What role does the law in this latter sense have in our lives? Basically, there are in theory two ways to be saved. We can keep the whole of God's law perfectly and so earn our own salvation. Or we can accept the sacrifice of Christ who died for our sins and kept the law perfectly for us. The latter is known as justification by faith alone. It is only faith in Jesus that saves us. Not faith in Jesus plus our good works or our keeping the law.

It would be worth your while to read the whole of Paul's letter to the Galatians. It is an unusual letter because of all his letters it is the only one which does not commend the church. Instead he goes straight to the point – his astonishment that they were so quickly turning from the grace of Christ to something which was really no gospel at all. They were basically adding the law to the gospel and thus creating a new gospel. Paul tells us that we are not saved by the law and we do not receive the Spirit by the law. So what is its purpose? Firstly, it is a schoolmaster to bring us to Christ. If we rely on the law we end up being under a curse – because none of us can keep it and as a result the Law condemns us. The law acted as a kind of guardian for us until Christ came and now we live by faith. When we come to faith in Christ we now live in the new way of the Spirit, not the old way of the written code.

Does this mean that the law has no place in the Christian life as some Christians would argue? They believe that because we live by faith and are under grace we don't need God's law at all. This is what we call 'anti-nomianism' (against the law). Others go the opposite extreme and would suggest that we are under law – this is what we call legalism. Paul provides us with a different and more balanced perspective. We are not under the law but we have been set free to obey God. We cannot be saved by keeping the Mosaic Law, and we cannot be sanctified (made holy) by keeping the Mosaic Law. However, this is not to say that there is no law, rules or principles in the Christian life. Even in Galatians, Paul warns us about 'the acts of the flesh', disunity and unrighteousness. Christians are not set free to sin; we are set free to serve.

What the law does is show us the standards and purity of God. Having been born again our desire is to please him and so walking in the new way of the Spirit, means that God's law is written on our hearts. We can learn from the Pentateuch; we read the law of Christ as given to us, for example, in the *Sermon on the Mount;* we see the high standards of holiness and the practical outworkings in the New Testament letters and our heart's desire is that God's will would be done on earth as it is in heaven. The role of the law is to educate, tutor, enlighten, but it cannot save or sanctify. However, those who are saved and those who are being made holy will seek to keep God's purest standards.

CONSIDER: Why is it foundational to the Christian life to understand the role of the Law? What is the difference between law and grace? What can we do to avoid the dangers of both anti-nomianism and legalism?

RECOMMENDED FURTHER READING:

A Little Book on the Christian Life – John Calvin

40 Questions About Christians and Biblical Law – Tom Schreiner

PRAYER: Be good to your servant while I live,
   that I may obey your word.
   Open my eyes that I may see
   wonderful things in your law (Psalm 119:17-18).

50. CHURCH, SALVATION AND HYPOCRISY

QUESTION: If I believe in God but don't go to church, will I still be saved? Why do Christians say one thing and do another?

BIBLE READING: Acts 2:42-47

TEXT: They devoted themselves to the apostles' teaching and to fellowship, to the breaking of bread and to prayer (Acts 2:42).

There is a growing trend in some parts of the Western Church to argue for churchless Christianity. St Augustine would have struggled with this novel idea:

'He who does not have the Church for his mother, cannot have God for his Father.'[29] It's partly based on a truth. We are not saved because we go to church, just as we are not saved by

---

29. Attributed to St Augustine of Hippo A.D. 354-430.

good works. But if we are saved we will do good works and if we are saved we are part of the Church.

Part of the problem here is again with definition. Have you noticed how in this book we have continually needed to define what we mean? This is because clear answers need clear questions. Your question speaks about going *to* church. What does that mean? To many it means the building – they are wrong. The view of church as building has no justification in the terms of the New Testament. The term church is from the Greek *ecclesia* which means 'the assembly'. The church is first of all something that we *are*, not something that we go to. The church is the whole body of Christ throughout the whole world, throughout all ages. That is what we call the universal church. We are baptised into that Church. We are part of it when we become believers. In that sense, you cannot be a Christian without being part of the Church, without being part of the body of Christ.

But the Bible also speaks of local churches (Galatians 1:1-2 or the seven churches in Revelation 2 and 3) – that is the local gathering of believers and their families. There is little evidence for the use of the term 'church' to describe a denomination – although many Christians would see that New Testament churches were not isolated and did act together as one body.

There is, however, a sense in which church is something that we both belong to and go to – when we gather together with the local congregation. Do you need to do that? Do you need to belong to a local church in order to be a Christian? This is a bit like baptism – you don't need to be baptised to be a Christian, but a Christian (a follower of Christ) will be baptised because they are following him. A very few people, like the thief on the cross, don't have the opportunity to be baptised, but these are exceptions. And exceptions make bad rules. The bottom line is that we are commanded to meet together and not to be isolated Christians, or just to gather with people we like.

And let us consider how we may spur one another on toward love and good deeds, not giving up meeting together, as some are in the habit of doing, but encouraging one another—and all the more as you see the Day approaching (Hebrews 10:24-25).

'*For where two or three gather in my name, there am I with them*' (Matthew 18:20).

'*Let the message of Christ dwell among you richly as you teach and admonish one another with all wisdom through psalms, hymns, and songs from the Spirit, singing to God with gratitude in your hearts*' (Colossians 3:16).

Why would you as a Christian, not want to meet with other Christians? Why would you not want to obey Christ? Why would you not want to be taught God's Word? Sing his praise? Join together in prayer? Evangelise with his people? Have fellowship with your brothers and sisters who you are going to spend all eternity with?

Because the church is full of hypocrites and is not perfect? Sometimes I am told, 'I can't go to church because it's full of hypocrites', to which the most obvious response is 'you should come, you would be very much at home!' The Bible tells us that every church is filled with sinners, including the pastors, elders and deacons. It will not be perfect. As C.H. Spurgeon said to a woman who was leaving his church because it was not perfect; 'Madam, when you find the perfect church, don't join it. You will only spoil it!' [30]

---

30. Attributed to C.H Spurgeon 1834-1892.

Christians (including you and I) say one thing and do another because we are sinful. That is not to excuse our sin – nor to say that there are not fake Christians and false teachers within the Church. Sadly this has been the way since the New Testament. But God is working out his purposes through his church and there is a great deal of reality, truth and beauty within it. For you to stay away from it is to harm both yourself and the church.

CONSIDER: Why would a Christian not want to go to a church? What should we look for in a church? How do we deal with hypocrisy within the church and ourselves?

RECOMMENDED FURTHER READING:
Why Bother with Church? – Sam Allberry

PRAYER: Lord Jesus, I thank you for your church – glorious as she is throughout the ages and even more glorious in heaven. I thank you for the hundreds of thousands of local churches throughout the world today and that you are continuing to build and increase your church through them. Lord, protect your church and lead me to serve in one that is faithful to you and your Word. Amen.

51. THE BEST CHURCH

QUESTION: What is the best church to attend? Is it bad if I enjoy football games more than church services?

BIBLE READING: Ephesians 4:1-16

TEXT: Instead, speaking the truth in love, we will grow to become in every respect the mature body of him who is the head, that is, Christ. From him the whole body, joined and held together by every supporting ligament, grows and builds itself up in love, as each part does its work (Ephesians 4:15-16).

The young man wanted to really push me. 'Would you go to church if you were not a minister?' 'Yes – I love going to church ... it's my life blood ... it's the greatest thing I do every week'. 'If you were given the choice of going to watch your football team in the cup final or going to church, what would you do?' 'I would go to church'. 'You're a fanatic!' This young man regularly travelled over 300 miles every second weekend and spent every spare penny he had on following his team – a group of men who kicked a ball around a pitch for ninety minutes – and he called me a fanatic!

I guess we pay for what we value and we spend time on what we value. I have been in church services which have been a lot less enjoyable than a football match – and I have been in football games which make the most miserable church service seem entertaining (you have to remember I am a Dundee and Scotland fan!). Let me ask the question another way – would it be bad if you enjoyed football games more than your family or your girlfriend/boyfriend? It is possible to enjoy both, but one is surely far more important than the other. Likewise with football and church – you can enjoy both, but only one will be of lasting benefit. God *richly provides us with everything for our enjoyment*' (1 Timothy 6:17), but we need to remember to worship the giver and not the gifts. Beware of turning sport (or any of God's good gifts) into an idol. Our God is a jealous God.

Let's come on to the second part of the question. What is the best church to go to? It's not a competition and I don't think we should be tied to a particular denomination but given that there are often a confusing number of churches, each claiming to be the church of Christ (if not the best) how do we know? In some areas you will be spoilt for choice in finding a good church, in others they will be as rare as hen's teeth!

What should you look for in a church? Too often we look at relatively superficial things – do we like the style of the music? Or the people? Is the building comfortable and convenient? What is the coffee like? This is consumer Christianity and it is an abomination – to use a good old-fashioned biblical word!

The Church is the Bride of Christ and we should expect certain things of any biblical church.

Firstly, there should be the preaching and teaching of the Word of God. To have a church without that is like having a restaurant with no food. To have a church which mixes the truth with false doctrine is like having a restaurant that serves poison. To have a church with only superficial teaching full of clichés and only a notional connection with the Bible is like getting your daily diet from a fast food restaurant when you could have steak! Make sure your church is a church that seeks to proclaim, sing, pray and live the Word of God.

In this latter respect, you are looking for a church that practices what it preaches. Having the right doctrine without the right practice is hypocrisy. For that reason I would look for a church where I could serve - even in the humblest capacity. Then I would always look for a church that I would be happy inviting my non-Christian friends to. And one that seeks to be a witness to and in the local community as well as supporting the wider church.

A church is not a church without baptism and the Lord's Supper - the sacraments. Different Christians have different beliefs about these but you do not have a church if you do not have them. And then there is church discipline. That doesn't sound nice. What does it mean? A young man called Robert Murray McCheyne became a very famous minister because although he was only a minister of his church, St Peter's in Dundee, for seven years before he died aged twenty-nine in 1843, he saw great blessing - including hundreds of young people coming to know the Lord. He wrote this: 'From that hour a new light broke in upon my mind, and I saw that if preaching be an ordinance of Christ, so is church discipline. I now feel deeply persuaded that both are of God - that two keys are committed to us by Christ, the one the key of doctrine, by means of which we unlock the treasures of the Bible, the other the key of discipline, by which we open or shut the way to the sealing ordinances of the faith. Both are Christ's gift, and neither is to be resigned without sin.'[31]

You and I both need a church with discipline – because we both need discipline. Can you imagine a football team without discipline? Where each player did what they wanted and ignored the manager, captain, referee, their teammates and the rules! It would destroy the team and end their career. We need discipline but it needs to be biblical discipline – not authoritarianism or cult like leadership. We need to be in churches where people will love us enough to pastor us, care for us and discipline us.

CONSIDER: What do you look for in a church? Is it ever right to leave a church? When would it be wrong to leave a church? Should church be enjoyable?

RECOMMENDED FURTHER READING:
Awakening – The Life of Robert Murray McCheyne – David Robertson

PRAYER: Lord, I confess that sometimes I find church dead-boring and I don't want to go. Lord, is it me? If it is, please work in me and change me. If it is not, then I ask you to change, restore and revive your church. Please lead me to a church that will honour you, teach me your Word and enable me to serve and praise you, in Jesus name. Amen.

---

31. Robert Murray McCheyne and Andrew A. Bonar, *Memoir and Remains of the Rev. Robert Murray McCheyne* (Edinburgh; London: Oliphant Anderson & Ferrier, 1894), 79–81.

52. KNOWING GOD'S WILL AND LOVE

QUESTION: How can I know the decisions I make are God's will? How can I know that God loves me?

BIBLE READING: Romans 12:1-21

TEXT: Do not conform to the pattern of this world, but be transformed by the renewing of your mind. Then you will be able to test and approve what God's will is—his good, pleasing and perfect will (Romans 12:2).

This is a great last question to finish with. It ties in with other questions in this book like no. 1 and no. 13. Indeed it is the whole purpose of this book. Knowing God, knowing his will and knowing his love.

As I hope you have seen throughout this book, the Bible does not give us a list of do's and don'ts. Instead we are given understanding about God, the church and ourselves. Christianity is not a computer programme, a moral code

215

or a 'how to self help' philosophy. It's about a relationship with God. The key to any relationship is communication. We communicate with God through prayer and he communicates with us through his Word. What we have tried to do in this book is to show how thinking biblically about issues can help bring clarity. What is vital is that we read our cultures and our lives through the lens of the Word of God, rather than reading the Word of God through the lens of our culture and lives.

A Christian is someone who is in Christ. As we grow in our faith and our relationship with him then that will result in a renewed mind. As we are transformed more and more into the likeness of Christ then we will be able to test and approve God's will.

But many of the questions we have looked at question whether that will is good. It is good, pleasing and perfect, but we fear that it may be bad, displeasing and imperfect. We need to face up to this. If God loves me then everything else falls into place. So how do we know God loves us? Listen to what he says.

'For God so loved the world that he gave his one and only Son, that whoever believes in him shall not perish but have eternal life. For God did not send his Son into the world to condemn the world, but to save the world through him' (John 3:16-17).

'I have been crucified with Christ and I no longer live, but Christ lives in me. The life I now live in the body, I live by faith in the Son of God, who loved me and gave himself for me' (Galatians 2:20).

I need nothing more than the cross of Christ to know how much God loves me. And if he has given me Christ then how will he not also, along with him, freely give us all things?

'Who shall separate us from the love of Christ? Shall trouble or hardship or persecution or famine or nakedness or danger or sword?

As it is written: "For your sake we face death all day long;
we are considered as sheep to be slaughtered"'

No, in all these things we are more than conquerors through him who loved us. For I am convinced that neither death nor life, neither angels nor demons, neither the present nor the future, nor any powers, neither height nor depth, nor anything else in all creation, will be able to separate us from the love of God that is in Christ Jesus our Lord (Romans 8:36).

CONSIDER: this wonderful Question and Answer from *The Heidelberg Catechism* (1):

Q. What is your only comfort in life and death?
A. That I am not my own,
but belong with body and soul,
both in life and in death,
to my faithful Saviour Jesus Christ.
He has fully paid for all my sins
with his precious blood,
and has set me free
from all the power of the devil.
He also preserves me in such a way
that without the will of my heavenly Father
not a hair can fall from my head;
indeed, all things must work together
for my salvation.
Therefore, by his Holy Spirit
he also assures me
of eternal life
and makes me heartily willing and ready
from now on to live for him.

RECOMMENDED FURTHER READING:

Newton on the Christian Life: To Live is Christ – Tony Reinke
(Of course the one book that we should all read every day, and base our lives on, is the Bible. Please don't take it for granted or assume that you know it. I have been studying, reading and praying the Bible for over forty years and I am still learning new things every week!)

PRAYER: For this reason I kneel before the Father, from whom every family in heaven and on earth derives its name. I pray that out of his glorious riches he may strengthen you with power through his Spirit in your inner being, so that Christ may dwell in your hearts through faith. And I pray that you, being rooted and established in love, may have power, together with all the Lord's holy people, to grasp how wide and long and high and deep is the love of Christ, and to know this love that surpasses knowledge—that you may be filled to the measure of all the fullness of God' (Ephesians 3:14-19).

AND FINALLY

Thanks for getting this far. Maybe you have further questions and would like another book (I hope to write one for teenagers who are not Christians but want to find out more – *Seek!*). I would suggest you ask your church, pastors, youth group leaders, teachers, parents or friends. If you would like to ask me then write me on (theweeflea@gmail.com).

Thanks to all who helped with this book – including my own church, St Peters in Dundee, who granted me a three month sabbatical to complete it. Thanks to the good Christians of Sydney who have welcomed myself and my wife Annabel with open arms, homes, churches and hearts. Especially St Thomas' Anglican (with their senior pastor, Simon Manchester and his wife Kathy) whose hospitality made all this possible. Thanks to their large youth group who gave me a really stimulating couple of Q and A sessions. Thanks also to Moore College for making this stray Presbyterian a visiting scholar and allowing me the use of their wonderful facilities. There are numerous others to thank but especially all the teenagers who wrote in with hundreds of questions from all over the world. I'm sorry if I haven't been able to include yours but I hope that the book will prove helpful to you nonetheless. Thanks also to the congregation of St Peters in Dundee and especially the young people who are like children to me!

I remain forever grateful to my wife Annabel and our growing family. This book is dedicated to two of them – our Australian granddaughter, Isla, and Scottish grandson, Finlay. May the Lord grant that by the time they are teenagers our respective societies will be changed and renewed by the gospel.

To God be the glory,
David Robertson

APPENDIX
RECOMMENDED BOOKS

1. *From the Mouth of God* – Sinclair B. Ferguson

2. *Why Trust the Bible?* – Amy Orr-Ewing

3. *God's Big Picture* – Vaughan Roberts

4. *Serving* Without Sinking - John Hindley

5. *Looking for God in Harry Potter* – John Granger

6. *Psalms – The Prayer Book of the Bible* – Dietrich Bonhoeffer

7. *Seven Days that Shook the Earth* – John Lennox

8. *God's Undertaker* – John Lennox

9. *Crazy Love* – Francis Chan

10. *The Dawkins Letters* – David Robertson

11. *Knowing God* – J.I. Packer

12. *Delighting in the Trinity* – Michael Reeves

13. *Discovering God's Will* – Sinclair B. Ferguson

14. *Walking with God through Pain and Suffering* – Tim Keller

15. *The Cross of Christ* – John Stott
    The Lion, the Witch and the Wardrobe – C.S. Lewis

16. *Magnificent Obsession* – David Robertson

17. *Assurance – Overcoming the Difficulty of Knowing Forgiveness* – John Owen

18. *God, That's not Fair* – Dick Dowsett
    Crucial Questions about Hell – Ajith Fernando

19. *Holiness* – J.C. Ryle

20. *Creation Care: A Biblical Theology of the Natural World* – Douglas Moo

21. *A Relentless Hope - Surviving the Storm of Teen Depression -* Gary Nelson

22. https://www.desiringgod.org/articles/what-about-those-who-have-never-heard - John Piper

23. *How will the World End?* - Jeramie Rinne

24. *Jesus Among Other Gods (Youth Edition)* - Ravi Zacharias.

25. *Desiring God* - John Piper

26. *Money Counts* - Graham Benyon

27. *Basic Christianity* - John Stott

28. *The Reason for God* - Tim Keller

29. *Hitler's Religion - The Twisted Beliefs that Drove the Third Reich* - Richard Weikart

30. *Mary Slessor: A Life on the Altar for God* - Bruce McLennan

31. *The Korean Pentecost* - Bruce Hunt and William Blair

32. *Love your Enemies* - John Piper

33. *Is God Anti-Gay?* - Sam Allberry
    Married for God - Christopher Ash

34. *Finally Free: Fighting for Purity With The Power of Grace -* Heath Lambert.

    Closing the Window, Steps to Living Porn-Free - Tim Chester.

35. *Revolution of Love and Balance* - George Verwer
    Seeking Allah, Finding Jesus - Nabeel Qureshi

36. *Transgender* - Vaughan Roberts

    When Harry met Sally - Ryan T. Anderson

37. *The Freedom of Self-Forgetfulness* - Tim Keller

38. *The Bruised Reed* - Richard Sibbes

39. *Prayer - Experiencing Awe and Intimacy with God* - Tim Keller
    The Valley of Vision - Arthur G. Bennett

40. *If God Already Knows – Why Pray?* – Douglas Kelly
    How Prayer Impacts Lives – Ed. Catherine Mackenzie

41. *Anxious for Nothing* – John Macarthur

42. *12 Ways Your Phone is Changing You* – Tony Reinke

43. *The Holiness of God* – R.C. Sproul

44. *Indwelling Sin in Believers* (abridged and made easy to read)
    – John Owen

45. *Life Interrupted: The Scoop on Being a Young Mom* – Tricia
    Goyer

46. *Principles of Conduct: Aspects of Biblical Ethics* – John Murray
    Knowing God's Will – M. Blaine Smith

47. *The Ten Commandments* – J. Douma

48. *Dealing with Depression* – Sarah Collins and Jane Haynes
    The Big Ego Trip – Glenn Harrison
    Eating Disorders – Emma Scrivener

49. *A Little Book on the Christian Life* – John Calvin
    40 Questions About Christians and Biblical Law – Tom
    Schreiner

50. *Why Bother with Church* – Sam Allberry

51. *Awakening – The Life of Robert Murray McCheyne* – David
    Robertson

52. *Newton on the Christian Life: To Live is Christ* – Tony Reinke

CHRISTIAN FOCUS PUBLICATIONS

Christian Focus | Christian Heritage | CF4K | Mentor

Christian Focus Publications publishes books for adults and children under its four main imprints: Christian Focus, CF4K, Mentor and Christian Heritage. Our books reflect our conviction that God's Word is reliable and Jesus is the way to know him, and live for ever with him.

Our children's publication list includes a Sunday school curriculum that covers pre-school to early teens, and puzzle and activity books. We also publish personal and family devotional titles, biographies and inspirational stories that children will love.

If you are looking for quality Bible teaching for children then we have an excellent range of Bible stories and age-specific theological books.

From pre-school board books to teenage apologetics, we have it covered!

Find us at our web page:
www.christianfocus.com

CF4•K
Because you're never
too young to know Jesus